Y0-BCW-857

AHEAD OF MYSELF

Confessions of a Professional Psychic

SHAWN ROBBINS
as told to Milton Pierce

Prentice-Hall, Inc. Englewood Cliffs, N.J.

To my loving parents, Birdye and Ruby,
for being there during the good
and bad times of my life

Ahead of Myself: Confessions of a Professional Psychic
by Shawn Robbins as told to Milton Pierce

Address inquiries to Prentice-Hall, Inc., Englewood Cliffs, N.J. 07632.

Printed in the United States of America

Prentice-Hall International, Inc., London
Prentice-Hall of Australia, Pty. Ltd., Sydney
Prentice-Hall of Canada, Ltd., Toronto
Prentice-Hall of India Private Ltd., New Delhi
Prentice-Hall of Japan, Inc., Tokyo
Prentice-Hall of Southeast Asia Pte. Ltd., Singapore
Whitehall Books Limited, Wellington, New Zealand

10 9 8 7 6 5 4 3 2 1

Library of Congress Cataloging in Publication Data

Robbins, Shawn.
Ahead of myself.

Includes index.

1. Robbins, Shawn. 2. Psychical research—United States—Biography. I. Pierce, Milton, joint author. II. Title.
BF1027.R56A32 133.3'092'4 [B] 80-20486
ISBN 0-13-004002-9

Contents

Part One

A Very Special Talent

1

What Does It Feel Like to Be Psychic

Click!

The camera shutter opens. In an instant, the camera is able to "see" a moment of life. In a split second, the film records a scene that never existed before—and never will again.

My name is Shawn Robbins. I am a professional psychic. In many ways, this psychic ability I have is like that camera. Something inside me is able to "see" beyond the normal world. Some hidden shutter opens and, for an instant, I am able to envision another dimension.

I am often asked to describe the process involved in making a prediction. People expect a simple, uncomplicated statement about how the experience feels or tastes or smells. But for questions like these, there are no simple answers. A prediction has many facets and takes many forms.

My Night Visions

Think about your dreams. Some are probably quite delightful—joyous times with special loved ones, or secret longings you wouldn't even want to admit. Other dreams are frightening, filled with anxieties, problems, fears, and long-suppressed emotions. Such dreams can leave you troubled for days afterward. Some people spend every night of their lives suffering recurrent dreams that cause them great pain.

For a moment imagine that, added to this kind of dream, you occasionally experienced a different, more powerful vision at night. In your sleep, you were suddenly transported to another place and time, where you experienced death and tragedy. And this would not be a simple dream, disappearing after only a few moments; it is closer to reality than dreaming. It is so real that you know either it *has* already happened or it *will* happen soon. The impending disaster is so real that it makes you want to run out and warn the world.

But worst of all, you are completely alone in the experience. No one else alive has shared this horrible vision. And should you try to warn anyone, no one will believe you. This is what my nights are like; this is the kind of dream that I and many other psychically gifted people have all the time.

An Uneasy Feeling...

It began one evening in 1974. I had just completed a fairly light day, having seen only one or two people for psychic readings. I was alone in my apartment, as usual, reading yet another book of nonfiction. After I read for a while, I began to feel uneasy. Something was nagging at me, preventing me from relaxing, as though my mind was trying to remind me of some forgotten chore or errand.

Yet, try as I might, I could not find the source of this strange sensation. I tried to think back over the predictions I had made for clients that day. Perhaps one of them was bothering me? Maybe I'd given a false prediction? But no answers emerged. I began to wonder if I was coming down with something. Or was there perhaps some message coming to me through ESP from a friend or client? I made myself as receptive as possible to any thoughts that someone might be aiming at me—and still, nothing.

It was now getting late, and after getting ready for bed, I lay down and tried to clear my mind of all the day's problems. Yet I still could not relax and become drowsy. Would this be one of those nights when sleep never seems to come? I tossed and turned for a while, and considered getting up to eat something.

Exactly what happened next I can't say with certainty. I

must have finally fallen asleep, because within a few moments I was dreaming. But this was no normal dream. It was a psychic dream experience. I had been having such dreams since my youth, and so it was quite easy to recognize.

Fog...and Bright Light

Like all other psychic dreams I've had since, the dream began with a dense, heavy fog. Then a few dominant objects appeared, brightly illuminated so that I couldn't help but see them. This time, it was an airplane.

Suddenly I was aboard, and recognized the interior of the plane as that of a DC-10. As I looked around me, I noticed that it was filled almost to capacity. Glancing around, I somehow instantly knew some of the passengers' names. They did not speak to me, and yet I knew them just the same.

Then I realized what was happening. The plane was about to crash. The passengers—laughing, talking, or sleeping a moment before—were now overcome with fear. The emotional pain was simply unbearable. All these people, struggling desperately to cling to life, were absolutely helpless to defend themselves. It was as though they all wanted to get out of their seats and somehow *hold* the plane up in the air, such was their desire to stay alive. But death was inevitable, and I sensed that all the passengers knew this. The level of pain and terror rose as each person realized that his or her life was about to end.

I could feel the crash coming, and then I sensed the physical shock of the impact with earth. I saw the bodies being thrown about the plane's interior. I could hear bones shattering as the giant steel machine was ripped into small, blazing sections.

And at that moment, I also "died," along with the other passengers. I was now aware of even more names and identities among those dying. Soon I was standing outside the plane, looking back at those dead and dying amidst the rubble. It was now that I saw the date and time appear before me in the air.

And suddenly I woke. It was like coming out of the most terrible, most realistic nightmare a person could experience. My whole body was trembling with fear. I was perspiring and felt as if I had a fever. And for a few seconds, I believed I *was* dead. But then I realized I had just experienced the most powerful psychic dream of my life. Quickly I ran for a pad and pencil to write down the details of the dream, including the flight, the time, and the names of some of the passengers on board.

The date that had appeared in my dream was almost exactly two weeks away. I had two weeks to stop this tragedy from occurring.

The rest of the night, I could not fall back asleep. I did not even wish to, terrified that the dream of destruction might return once my eyes closed, and so I forced myself to stay awake. And yet at the same time, I also felt a sense of peace—somehow, the inexplicable anxiety I had experienced all evening was now gone. Now the dream had occurred, the story had been told, and the nervous anticipation was gone.

I Warn the FBI

The next morning I wasted no time; I did not even stop to wonder if the authorities would believe my story. People had to be warned, even if they laughed at me and paid no attention. This was not the kind of prediction I could keep to myself.

I called the FBI office in New York and was soon put in touch with a friendly officer. Although I sensed that he thought I was probably crazy, he was kind enough to take down all the details of my dream as I related them to him. He said he would pass the information along to the right people, and thanked me for my trouble and interest. I did not know if anyone besides that officer would ever hear of this dream, but I was happy just to have reached *someone* to issue a warning.

I am still not sure if that FBI officer ever passed on the message. But in any event, the plane was not grounded. Two weeks later, at the exact time I had foreseen, a DC-10 did indeed crash.

When the list of the victims appeared in the paper, I saw that all the names I had given the FBI officer were included—as of course were the names of many, many more.

I had lived through this horrible dream, and though I now knew that finally my gift could do good for a large number of people, I still felt frightened by the dream—and proud of it, since, had it only been heeded, it might have saved many lives.

This was a tremendously frustrating experience. I had predicted disaster, warned that it was coming, and yet no one had paid any attention whatsoever. What good was my gift, I wondered, if no one bothered to listen?

I began to doubt myself, wondering if I could have done more. Should I have called the airlines? They would have paid even less attention than the FBI. Should I have contacted the individuals whose names I had seen in the dream? But this would have been a little like yelling "Fire!" in a crowded theater. I simply couldn't begin to frighten people that way.

I was beginning to question my whole decision to become a professional psychic. If I could never *really* help anyone, I would feel as isolated as I had back in high school—one person, alone in the world, who could never hope to be understood.

Recognition

A few days later I received a call from a reporter at the *National Enquirer*'s offices. Somehow he had heard about my call to the FBI. Perhaps he had a friend there who had noticed my phone call and realized it simply could not be a coincidence.

Soon the *Enquirer* ran a story about my prediction of the DC-10 crash. And within a few weeks I was receiving a mass of mail from *Enquirer* readers. The paper began to ask me more and more questions and to publish some of my predictions. And after a short time, the *Enquirer* added my name to its list of the ten top psychics.

This power I have—this psychic ability by which I make my living—is something that I cannot fully understand. I do not think it has anything to do with religion, in the conventional sense. I do not think it has anything to do with good or evil, in the way that we comprehend good and evil. I do not believe it can be commanded or controlled.

There is so much that I do not understand: Why do I have this gift? Why am I able to see things that other people cannot? Is this power something I can share with other people, something that can be developed? Is it possible that at some time in the future, all people will have this same ability?

Click! A shutter opens. And in a flash, I am able to see that five hundred people will die in a plane crash. Click! And I see where a murderer has hidden the body of his victim. Click! And I can see that a certain stock will double in value over the next three months.

Why have I been given this gift? What does it really mean? Why do so many charlatans and profiteers want to exploit my abilities? When I am able to see into the future, what really happens? How does this power work? What is the force that I am unable to control?

I am able to do things and see things that other people cannot. I do not understand how this happens, or for what reason. But there are some things that I do understand. And I want to share them with you. I have written them down, as honestly and directly as I can.

This is my story.

2
First Experiences

Being psychic does not change the bond between parent and child. If anything, it enhances it.

Much of what I am today—including my powers, success, problems, and personality—comes directly from my upbringing.

My Mother—Born With a Veil Over Her Face

My mother was born in Brooklyn, New York, in 1918. At birth, her face was covered by a thin film of tissue. The old wives tale says this relatively rare occurrence, being born with a veil over the face, is the sign of a special gift, usually clairvoyance.

Indeed this omen proved true. My mother did possess psychic powers; in fact, in a small way, she was herself a professional psychic.

Her mother owned Orchard Grove, a small hotel in the Catskill Mountains, where she lived all year round. Of course, the resort mountains outside New York City were not so developed in those days. This was the country, complete with outhouses and dirt roads.

My mother did many chores around the hotel—housekeeping, kitchen work—making sure guests were comfortable and entertained. Even in winter she would walk five miles every day to town over snow-covered roads, carrying groceries, supplies—even live poultry!

But perhaps her most important task was that of reading the guests' palms. They would ask her many of the same questions my clients ask me today: When will I marry? What career should I choose? What will my future be like? And the majority of my mother's predictions were accurate.

But she soon came to fear (just as I would) that she was not simply foreseeing the future, but, in some way, she was also making things happen. Since a tragic prediction can truly make one feel a deep sense of guilt, my mother decided to shun the psychic life forever.

My Father—Artistic and Psychic

My father was born in 1916, also in Brooklyn. Soon after, his family returned to Russia. He too is psychic, and says at night he often saw ghosts wandering through the dark forests of Russia.

Once back in America, he spent most of his spare time fixing and repairing things for friends and neighbors, and he taught Latin at a Brooklyn school. Despite his knowledge of languages and his musical talents, my dad wound up going into the tool and die industry, creating products to serve the jewelry trade. Eventually he acquired his own company and became a full-fledged entrepreneur.

Marriage and Children

When my mother was 19 and my dad 21, they met each other at a social-club dance in Brooklyn.

My mother tells me that from the first moment she saw my father, she sensed that they would always be together. My dad say he felt the same. They married, and after a few years my sister was born. I came along about four years later. My parents believed deeply in psychic power, and fully expected me to possess the gift of "unseen knowledge." But while they assumed that I too would be gifted, they did not want me to develop my powers.

Seven Pounds, Two Ounces... and Psychic

My mother moved slowly, resting her weight on my father, letting his strength support her. His left arm was gently holding her waist, his right controlled the umbrella that protected them both from the cold, driving rain. As my mother stepped through the steel doorway and into the hospital reception area, she said, "A girl—with brown hair and hazel eyes."

Taking her first breath of hospital air, dense with the smell of medicine, illness, and disinfectant, she added, "Seven pounds, two ounces."

My father did not stop to doubt her prediction. He knew that she could see what would be happening just a few minutes later in the delivery room. "Seven pounds, two ounces, and *psychic*, I suppose," he said quietly.

As they stepped toward the admissions desk, a middle-aged nurse in a heavily starched white uniform ran around the desk to aid my obviously pregnant mother.

"What else?" my mother whispered, and she and my father laughed quietly, secure in the knowledge that her vision would almost certainly come true.

Within minutes, my mother sat in a wheelchair, and was sped through the brightly lit hospital corridor. My father walked briskly alongside, not fully trusting the young intern with his delicate wife. He nervously searched for a few last words of advice to give his wife before she entered the then no-man's-land where babies were born.

"Rubin, just relax," my mother said, as another stabbing labor pain spread through her body. "Everything will be fine. I *know* that everything will be fine."

The wheelchair moved between the swinging doors of the delivery room, leaving my father behind, standing in the fluorescent light and listening to the chimes paging some doctor to surgery. Another nurse—an apparent duplicate of the admissions clerk—led him to the waiting room. There, other fathers were busy chain-smoking and desperately awaiting some word from inside.

Within half an hour, word did arrive. A pretty young nurse entered the waiting room, causing all four expectant fathers to jump up hopefully from their green leather chairs.

"Mr. Robbins?" inquired the nurse. The other fathers returned to their chairs, to their waiting and smoking. "It's a girl, Mr. Robbins. Seven pounds, two ounces. Your wife is fine, and the baby is healthy."

My father smiled. *And psychic,* he thought to himself.

And so I entered the world on a rainy day in 1945. Rubin and Birdye had their second daughter. New York City had another citizen.

And the world had another psychic.

Coming Home

My father's 1939 Dodge sedan came round the corner, moving at a leisurely pace past the small houses and toward our modest home. It was a pleasant, quiet street in Queens, New York, not opulent in any way, but comfortable and well kept. He stared directly ahead at the road, but from the corner of his eye he was hoping to see the neighbors, smiling and gossiping: *Here comes Mrs. Robbins, home from the hospital with her new baby.*

I was cradled in my mother's arms, wrapped in a clean pink blanket, wearing the little white cap she had knitted years before in anticipation of this day. Her heart was filled with a new mother's joy, a feeling of accomplishment at having fulfilled her life's goal. Perhaps she was dreaming of her daughter grown and married, and bringing her own family home for the holidays. Or she may have envisioned me as a famous actress or ballerina, bowing and holding flowers on the stage of Carnegie Hall.

But never could she have known that one day her daughter would be known to the world as Shawn Robbins, a professional psychic.

I wonder now if even then, after only five days of life, my eyes still unseeing, my mind was already traveling to places I had never been. Could I see my parents' thoughts, the joys and worries of this newborn responsibility? Did I already know who and what I would one day become? Like all babies, I had a sixth sense. I knew my mother without seeing her. I could feel the love in my parents' touch. But I was different from the other babies born that day in the hospital. Within my soul was a special gift, a *mysterious* ability to know the unknown and to see things that have not yet occurred. This power would grow as I did, strengthen as I did, until finally I would choose a path in life unlike any other—one that would bring me many added joys and pains, tears and frustrations.

My father pushed open the front door and carried me inside. My mother sat in her favorite chair, a wedding gift from my grandfather, and took me back into her embrace. My father went into the bedroom to get the new Kodak he had bought just for this occasion.

Filled with the wonder of a new life, my mother stroked my forehead lightly and hummed a lullaby. As I began to sense my surroundings—the emotions and personalities that reverberated from the walls of our humble home—my eyes slowly closed, and I began to dream. . . .

First Years' Joys—and Fears

In most ways my first years were like those of any other little girl. I believed in Santa Claus, played with dolls, and slept with a teddy bear. When I spilled my milk at the dinner table, my father got upset as all fathers do. And when I lay awake at night because of a nightmare, afraid to go back to sleep, my father would come to sit beside me, whispering in a low and soothing voice until I drifted off again.

I've spent many hours with my mother listening to stories and anecdotes, trying to piece together events of my early years.

For the most part, my childhood was not unusual, but rather a simple sequence of events—with smiles and tears, problems and pitfalls like those we all experience.

But I was not an average child. As I would learn later in life, my mother and father were both psychic. My sister Helene, four years older than I, had already shown some special powers. When I was born, my parents expected the same quality in me, and while they encouraged my sister and me to be unique and to develop our abilities, they had many fears for us as well.

Why Am I Psychic?

Many people have asked me how psychic powers are transferred. Personally, I put little faith in reincarnation. I am not in any position to deny the possibility that we have all lived many other lives before, but somehow I just feel that I'm unique, too individual to have been someone else. I think everyone feels this way. You may believe in reincarnation, but can you truly admit to yourself that you are not a completely unique individual, unrelated to anyone who may have lived thousands of years ago?

But I do believe that psychic power is hereditary, passed on through the mother. Of course some women can be born into a psychic family and not have psychic powers themselves, but I think these women bring it to the next generation. Many men are psychic—Edgar Cayce, for example—but I don't think a man passes along the power to his children. If his wife isn't psychic, his children probably won't be. My mother inherited her psychic powers from her mother, and I, in turn, inherited those powers from her.

Why does one person in this chain have more ability than another? I am not sure, but for one thing, psychic powers must be developed. They do not become strong and accurate unless exercised. Chances are that my sister could have been just as powerful a psychic as I—had she made the effort.

Secondly, I believe that, vital to developing this gift. is self-awareness, soul-searching, and self-examination. Even the strongest psychic impressions might never come through individuals who tend to be out of touch with their feelings.

Finally, I truly believe that my psychic powers are a gift from God. There must be a very important reason why I am a practicing psychic today while my sister is not. In her youth, my mother had made many predictions and had begun to develop very strong psychic abilities. But she was also intimidated by these experiences, feeling—as I would later—that sometimes she was not only foreseeing tragedy, but causing it, too. This fear led her to abandon the psychic life, although she continued to believe deeply in psychic phenomena and allowed my sister and me to use our gifts.

At the same time, she wanted us to enjoy a normal, healthy childhood. My parents tried to hide my psychic powers from our neighbors and friends, fearing that I would be laughed at. Well aware of the problems, responsibility, and loneliness that being psychic brings, they naturally wished to spare me any pains they could.

So as I grew—and my powers became stronger, my visions more frequent—my parents both understood and discouraged my abilities.

"Seeing" and Foreseeing

There were early signs of my growing abilities. Other mothers on our block would complain to each other about their children's habit of always misplacing toys. My mother would listen sympathetically, but would never completely understand the other women's frustrations.

"I guess I'm just lucky," she would tell them. "Shawn never loses *anything!* I don't know how she does it, but she always comes up with toys I thought she'd misplaced."

The consensus on the block was that I was a gifted child and a blessing to my parents. Only my parents knew the truth.

I have dim memories of finding things I'd lost. Somehow, I could just *see* them—behind the sofa, or at the back of an overstuffed drawer. In my mind's eye I could visualize exactly where that dolly's dress was. Then I would simply go to the place I had seen in my mind's eye and find the dress waiting for me.

I was quite pleased with myself at being able to find these missing things, but it never occurred to me that this was in any way unusual. Like other children, I was just beginning to distinguish between myself and the rest of the world, and I assumed that everyone else had the same powers. Not until several years later would I learn, with much pain and disappointment, that something about me was strange, mysterious, and frightening.

Many of my precognitions in those years were not nearly as pleasant as finding lost toys. Foreseeing trips to the doctor's office, I would cry for hours. Like every other child, I hated doctors. They would smile and tickle your chin, trying desperately to make you happy, while one hand remained behind their back, holding the hypodermic needle for an immunization shot. But the "friendly" act never worked for me. Every child knew the needle was coming sooner or later—but I could *see* the needle hidden behind his back!

Another time I was able to foresee that an outing to see a Disney cartoon would be cancelled. Even before she spoke, I could hear my mother saying, "Honey, we'll have to postpone seeing *Sleeping Beauty* until next week. Our budget is a little low right now. I'm sorry."

But my mother would never have to explain. I would have been crying for hours, heartbroken that our adventure was going to be cancelled.

In some way, perhaps this pain I suffered was useful: My parents had to break disappointing news to me only rarely. I almost always experienced my little tragedies before they actually occurred. Although my psychic powers have sometimes caused me unhappiness, I believe I have been able to do a lot of good with my gift. Accepting the pain and torment, particularly when I have a premonition of death, is part of the responsibility of being a psychic.

I have no way of knowing why I was chosen to be the most unusual girl in my neighborhood. I simply tried to use my gift to help others. In my parents' bedroom, back in the shadows of their closet, was an old, gray shoebox filled with photographs of my family and my parents' friends. I would often ask my mother to get that box out of the closet, and then spend hours staring at the pictures. The people always looked funny to me: men in bowler hats, boys in knickers, women wearing bathing suits that covered more than some dresses I now own.

Many of these people were already dead, but as I stared into their faces, I felt they were speaking to me; I could imagine what they were thinking. I could almost *hear* what they were saying to each other. Every face seemed strangely alive with desires and feelings and ideas. It was as though I knew these people myself. I now realize this was a psychic experience that probably helped me strengthen my powers, but at age three, it was simply a game.

How do you explain to a three-year-old that she has psychic power? How do you keep her from inspiring outrage when she starts making predictions at her playmates' houses? How do you keep her friends from thinking she is strange, conceited, or just plain crazy?

In a way, my parents' indecision often made me feel even more isolated and confused, but though I had times of doubt and pain, I always knew that their love for me was strong and that they accepted me exactly as I was.

The First Psychic Experience

My mother has told me that my first major psychic experience saved our home from burning. One night, while asleep, I began to cough. Soon the coughing turned to choking, and my mother rushed into the room to make sure I was all right.

"Daddy!" I cried, still half asleep.

"Daddy's downstairs, sweetheart," my mother replied. "Let me get you some water."

But I could not be calmed. "Fire!" I shouted, still choking, and beginning to cry. My mother had never seen me so upset and terrified before.

"What fire, Shawn? You're just having a bad dream." She leaned over and lifted me into her arms. "Let's go downstairs and get some fresh air, and then your dream will go away."

My mother carried me downstairs, but I continued to cry and choke, repeating "Daddy!" and "Fire!" over and over again. My father had been sitting in the living room, reading. When my mother looked into the living room, she noticed that my father had fallen asleep and the air was filling with smoke! (An electrical cord had apparently become exposed, and the rug was beginning to smolder.)

"Oh, my God!" my mother cried, placing me on the floor and running to awaken my father. When my father realized what was happening, he rushed us to the front lawn, then ran back in to put out the fire. My mother held me in her arms and we watched him pour water on the rug, now in flames. In a few minutes we went back in, opened the windows, and let out the billowing smoke. (Incredibly, my sister Helene slept through the entire incident.)

The next day my parents remarked on how I had awakened just as the fire began.

"Thank God you had that nightmare, little girl," my father said. "You might just have saved our lives last night."

I can now imagine exactly what I was dreaming that night: a complete premonition of what was about to happen. I had seen into the future and predicted tragedy for the first time. And fortunately the tragedy had been avoided.

No Surprises

There were certain advantages to being a psychic child. But incidents like that of the fire were few and far between. Most of the time I could simply tell what was about to happen, or guess what I might be doing a few days hence. I always knew what Santa had brought long before I ran downstairs Christmas morning. (Of course, having the true optimism only a child can have, I never questioned Santa Claus's existence!) I knew when my friends would come over or call me on the phone. I knew when my parents were planning a trip to Coney Island or to the park for ice-skating. And when I knew good times were coming, I still enjoyed them as any child would.

The ones who were deprived were my parents. Just as they seldom had to tell me bad news, so they rarely had the opportunity to surprise me.

My First Birthday Party

When my sixth birthday was drawing near, my parents were planning a surprise party for me. Weeks in advance they had begun sending out invitations and buying gifts for me.

"Can I invite all my friends to the party?" I asked one day. My mother looked stunned. Her face dropped. (I wonder if these parties are thrown for the children or for the adults.) "What party, Shawn?"

"The surprise party for my birthday."

"There's no party, honey. I didn't know you wanted one. Maybe next year, OK?" She tried not to show her disappointment. I sensed that I had somehow hurt my mother, so for the next few weeks I tried not to mention the party. But I knew she was still trying to fool me, and the thought of the party was exciting, so a question occasionally came out: "Are we going to play games at the party?"

"Shawn, I told you there is no party. Now stop it!"

Poor Mom! As my birthday drew closer, I told her that Missy, one of my favorite playmates, "cut her leg and it hurts real bad, so she can't come to my party".

"Shawn, I've told you over and over, *there is no party*! Besides, I just spoke with Missy's mother on the phone. Missy is sound asleep in bed, exactly where you should be right now!"

"I sure wish Missy could come. She's my bestest pal." That night I took myself to bed, regretting that my party had already lost its best guest.

The next day, I knew, Mom and Missy's mother planned to go shopping for a birthday present. I knew what they were thinking of getting me—but I also knew they wouldn't go shopping that day!

Later, Missy's mother telephoned: "I'm at the hospital."

"What happened?" asked my mother, alarmed.

"Oh, Missy fell on some glass and cut her leg. It was pretty bad for a while. She needed stitches."

"Oh, no!"

"Don't worry, she'll be fine. But until the stitches come out, she has to take it very easy."

My mother put down the phone and sat, staring at the kitchen table. Then she turned and gave me a strange look I had never seen before.

It frightened me a little. I thought perhaps she would get mad again.

But she simply stared at me as if she had never really seen me before. After a moment she got up, took me in her arms, and began to cry. My mother's expectations had come true, and although she was proud of my psychic gift, she feared the difficult life ahead of me.

The next day, my father took me to the zoo for the afternoon so that I'd be away from the house and the surprise could be readied. I think my mother was beginning to understand what was happening in my mind, but she carried out her long-planned surprise party anyway. Every detail was just as she'd planned, but she went one step further, she hid all my presents around the living room, to test if I could find them. (Our living room was by far the largest room in our house, so it wouldn't be easy for a little girl just turned six.)

When my father and I opened the front door, ten of my best friends shouted "Happy Birthday!" The living room was covered with pink and red and blue balloons, and streamers dangled from the ceiling and the bookcases.

"Everyone brought a present, ten altogether, and we hid them all around the room. Now you must try to find them!"

I thought this was the greatest game I'd ever played—especially since I knew I would win!

My mother tells me that I walked around the room like a little robot, going to the exact spots where the presents were hidden. Some presents were hidden in places I couldn't reach, so I just pointed and my father helped me. My guests began to wonder if I'd been watching through the window. Everyone likes to show off their talents, and I was no exception. People assumed I was just bright and had guessed the likely hiding places, but this wasn't the compliment I had been hoping for. At that very first birthday party I also learned that a psychic should never thank anyone for a gift until it has been opened. I found myself saying "Thanks for the coloring book, Cathy," before I'd taken off the wrapping paper. As my father reached for one present hidden on the china cabinet, I said, "Dad, be real careful. It's a real old dolly and it'll break easily."

My friend Shara let out a little shriek.

"Shawn!" my mother said, "who told you about that doll? It's not fair to Shara."

Out of the house ran Shara, crying with disappointment. I followed, trying to think of some way to explain. She wouldn't speak to me, though, and spent most of the party sulking under our apple tree. Later everyone, including Shara, had cake and ice cream; and like every healthy birthday girl, I ate myself sick!

Growing Up in a Changing World

I wonder if the other kids' mothers thought my parents set up that treasure hunt to make me look like a genius. I know our neighbors often suspected things about me, but my parents made quite a successful effort to conceal my powers, to spare me others' questions and condemnations.

In those days, most people considered psychic power something of a sideshow trick, restricted to gypsies and fortune-tellers. Many considered topics like astrology and ESP immoral and sacrilegious. So my parents tried at times to discourage my visions and feelings, fearing what society might think of me. This was a direct response to their own life experiences.

But in my home, psychic phenomena were common; we often communicated nonverbally. Lying was virtually impossible, and there were very few events that at least one of us had not predicted. In my family, *not* knowing the future was unusual!

Yet although there were occasional occurrences of childhood clairvoyance and telepathy, I spent most of my days like other children. I'd grudgingly walk to school each morning with my friends, carrying a few notebooks and a peanut butter and jelly sandwich. I sat in class, staring out the window at spring flowers or the fresh-fallen snow, never quite understanding why school was necessary. Soon I would realize that I was not like my friends or my teachers; the life they were preparing me for could never be mine. The road for me was the one less taken, filled with doubts and fears—a road I would have to walk alone.

3
Growing Up Psychic

My parents' method of raising children was quite unorthodox in many ways. To a large extent, they gave my sister and me more freedom than was given any other children I knew. Of course, we had established bedtimes, chores, and forbidden behavior. But in terms of our thoughts, pursuits, and interests, our parents allowed us complete self-determination. Though they exposed us to beautiful music, great works of art, fine literature, they didn't force us to play instruments or take dancing lessons as so many mothers and fathers do.

I spent days searching libraries and bookstores for books about psychic phenomena, for, once I became aware of my gift, I wanted to study the topic as much as possible. Yet knowing my mother worried about my powers, I did not want to bring these books home and thus cause her any unnecessary anguish.

My sister, too, had psychic powers she had developed over many years. But like my mother, she turned her back on her own gift. I can understand exactly how my mother and sister feel, but, perhaps because my gift is stronger, I cannot deny it when images are as strong as the ones that come to me.

At first the awareness of my psychic gifts was just a vague sense. I would awaken in the middle of the night, shaking with fear. "Did you have a nightmare?" my mother would ask.

"I'm not sure what it was." But somehow she knew what I was experiencing.

From time to time I would see people walking down the street, and realize that they were in trouble. It was a hard feeling to pinpoint, though. Let me give you a typical instance. My mother once sent me to the grocery store to get two quarts of milk. Mr. Stennis gave me the bottles.

"How's your arm?" I asked him.

"My arm?" He looked at me strangely. "There's nothing wrong with my arm..."

"Oh," I apologized. "I thought you told my mother there was."

"Nope, nothing wrong," he insisted.

The next day I heard that Stennis had slipped on some newly fallen snow and had broken his forearm.

Such glimpses into that other dimension took many forms, but always seemed to be a part of this reality. It was during this period of my life that I realized I was really different. It was also during this time that my gifts began to grow—and take control of my life.

At first I thought I was just having bad dreams. Teachers believed that I had a vivid imagination. Somehow I "remembered" things that did not take place until afterwards. . . . But the pattern became clear. I was seeing things that were about to take place, thinly disguised as memories or bad dreams. It is still difficult for me to distinguish between a psychic flash and reality.

I doubt any psychic has total control over this ability. In my opinion, those who claim they do are not being honest with themselves or with us.

During my eighth year I was finally able to fully understand the nature of the gift that made me different from everyone else.

"You Have the Gift..."

My grandmother was a very unusual woman. Strong, independent, and demanding, she was also filled with love and amazing loyalty. She too had psychic abilities, which I, in turn, inherited. One day when Grandma had come to visit us, she sat me down beside her on the living room sofa.

"Shawn," she said quietly, "you know that you are different, don't you?"

"How, Grandma?"

"You have the gift, child. You're a seer, a clairvoyant."

These words had no meaning for me, but I listened in fascination.

"You know things others don't," she continued. "You can see things before they happen. You can read what others are thinking, can't you, Shawn?"

"Sometimes I can. I thought everyone did."

"No, Shawn. You have a special gift from God that will grow stronger as you grow, and you will come to use it wisely. At one point you will deny this gift, fearing the problems it brings. But you will not be able to escape what God has planned for you. You will take up your burden and put it to good use to help other people with their problems."

"How do you know all this, Grandma?"

"I too have this gift, Shawn, but not like you. I can feel you are powerful, Shawn; I can see it in your eyes. You wait a few years, and see if what your old grandma says doesn't come true."

On a Saturday afternoon a few weeks later, I was out playing in the backyard with one of my friends. Suddenly I heard my grandmother's voice calling to me very faintly, saying "Good-bye, Shawn," and telling me she loved me and would someday see me again in heaven.

Terribly frightened, I tried not to cry as I left my friend in the yard and ran into the kitchen. My mother was just replacing the phone as I came in. She was crying a bit and seemed very upset.

"Mommy," I cried, "Grandma is going to heaven. Why is Grandma leaving?"

My mother had just been speaking with the doctor. "Grandma has gone to the hospital, honey, but she's going to be all right. How did you know Grandma was sick?"

"I just knew, Mommy. I heard Grandma tell me so."

After so many years of similar occurrences, my mother didn't seem shocked, but in her eyes there was a look that combined wonder at the strength of my gift and fear of what lay in store for me.

I knew my grandmother would *not* be all right. I knew that I would never see her on earth again.

A few hours later, the telephone call came. Grandma was dead.

Not until several days after the funeral did our life begin to return to normal. My mother didn't cry so often. We ended our mourning and began watching TV in the evenings again.

But my life would never be the same. I knew now, without question, that her words of prophecy were true. My mother understood too, although she would continue trying to hide things from me just the same. When I was about ten, my sister fell very ill with pneumonia. As I came home from school, my mother met me on the front lawn and explained that I would be going away for a few days to stay with relatives who lived nearby. Although she did not give a reason for my trip, I knew it was because my sister was sick. I asked her directly if my sister was going to be all right, but my mother denied that anything was wrong. I felt angry and hurt. Why did my parents lie to me? Only later did I realize that they were simply trying to spare me worry.

The Quiz

Like most kids, I hated going to school. I got in trouble for talking and fooling around during class, and I did as little homework as possible.

Being psychic had some advantages in the eighth grade. Sometimes things I said would impress people; other times the other kids would ostracize me and call me weird.

One day, instead of just daydreaming during a lecture, I tried to focus my thoughts on those of my teacher. As Mrs. Miller rattled on about George Washington and the American Revolution, I could hear her thinking, "You kids may not be interested now, but you'll be sorry during the quiz tomorrow!" She was also thinking about her family and what she would make for dinner that evening; and for the first time I realized that teachers were human like everyone else.

That night I amazed my mother by spending extra time studying American history. Doing my homework willingly was very uncharacteristic!

The next morning, before classes began, I sat in the schoolyard going over my history notes once more. All my friends were busy playing ball and flipping baseball cards.

"What ya doin'?" asked my good friend Shara. "Come on an' play with us."

"I gotta study. Mrs. Miller's gonna give a quiz today, and I don't know this stuff at all."

"How do you know that? She didn't say anything about a quiz."

"I just know, that's all."

"Did she tell you? *How* do you know about it?"

I was ready to tell Shara about reading Mrs. Miller's mind, but I reconsidered. Previously I had never hesitated to mention predictions and visions. But now I knew that these occurrences were so unusual that no one would believe my stories were true.

"How do you know she's giving a quiz?" Shara repeated.

"I just know, that's all. Take my word for it."

Before history class started, the rumor about the coming quiz had spread. By the time we got into Mrs. Miller's room, everyone was prepared.

"I hope you all paid attention to my lecture yesterday," she said, "because I'm giving a surprise quiz on that material right now."

Mrs. Miller waited for the groan of displeasure from the class, but it never came. The students all took out a piece of paper for their answers as though the quiz had been announced days before.

Shara glanced over at me in disbelief. I raised my eyebrows and shrugged my shoulders.

The next day during history class, Mrs. Miller reported that the quiz scores were unusually high, leading her to assume that everyone had paid close attention to her lecture on George Washington. But I knew she was really thinking that someone had cheated. The class had *known* the quiz was coming—but how? She hadn't discussed it with anyone. There were no memos referring to it in her desk for someone to sneak a look at. How had the students found out?

Before that day's class ended, Mrs. Miller confronted us. How had we found out about the quiz? A few people mentioned a rumor going around the morning before, and eventually that rumor was attributed to me. Mrs. Miller asked me to come see her after school.

I didn't need psychic powers to predict what Mrs. Miller wanted to talk to me about. I spent the rest of the afternoon debating whether I should admit having read her mind.

After the bell ending the school day had rung, my friends all hurried home while I dragged myself to Mrs. Miller's room. The halls were empty and silent as I knocked on the heavy wooden door. Mrs. Miller was seated at her desk, her horn-rimmed glasses perched on the end of her nose. She looked up at me as she graded papers.

"How did you know I planned that quiz, Shawn?"

The sixty-four-thousand-dollar question! Could I say, "I read your mind"?

"I just had a hunch, I guess."

She paused, staring coldly at me. "A hunch, eh? I see. It's too bad you didn't have more of a hunch about George Washington. Your grade was among the worst in the class."

I escaped punishment, but not a bad grade. For some reason, I could never "see" the answers to test questions.

My mother and father were both raised in very musical families. Mom studied opera in her youth with a great teacher by the name of Madame Kibits. My father was very fond of singing, and as a young man often entertained friends with his voice.

It was therefore not surprising that I learned to play the guitar, and my sister, the accordion. In our teens, we performed together for friends, at parties and club meetings, and even on local radio shows.

I believe there's a strong connection between the creative arts and psychic phenomena. Artists, writers, dancers, musicians, all possess some degree of psychic power, I think, because psychic visions and artistic creativity both spring from the same area of the soul. During those grade-school years I had a few close friends. But like most children, I had a new "best friend" every September. At the age of eleven or twelve, friendships don't last very long—especially when you're psychic.

By the age of twelve I knew what things I could predict, and was beginning to understand that none of my friends could see and know what I knew. I still had not even heard the word *psychic*, yet at times, I felt pleased that I was somehow better than my friends. At other times, I simply felt alone and isolated from everyone around me.

Within a few years my psychic nature made me a loner, virtually without any friends. I spent most of my days alone, reading or playing guitar. Although I tried not to bring my psychic abilities to my friends' attention, most of them eventually put two and two together. Sooner or later something would come out about my ability to read minds and make predictions, and most of my friends reacted negatively, thinking I was trying to act superior. The greatest sin for a twelve-year-old is to be conceited, and anyone with a special gift or talent is "stuck up." This anxiety and sadness would grow in the years to come until finally, in my teens, I would try to deny my gift, desperately hoping to avoid the life I was destined for.

A Vision of Death

Once, a close friend of mine came to my house crying over a dog she'd had for years. He'd gone out on the prowl the night before and had not returned.

She asked me if I would help her find her dog. I agreed, and we began searching the neighborhood. But, after a short while a vision came to me: Her dog was dead. I decided to tell her that prolonging the search seemed pointless.

Though I tried to break the news as gently as possible, naturally she was outraged, thinking I was being cruel. A few days later, however, the police called to say the dog had been found beside a highway dead.

That girl never spoke to me again. Chances are, she still blames me for her pet's death.

Events like this are common. Because psychics bear bad tidings, people think they cause misfortunes. I can understand this resentment, but it seems unfair. I do not cause tragedies to occur, I simply see them coming. In the years to come, my powers were going to lose me a lot of friends. Rumor would spread that I thought I could predict the future and read minds—and most of my peers considered me egotistical or insane.

The Ring

At home, my parents still tried to act as though I were just like everyone else. One day I came home from school to find my mother sitting in the kitchen, crying quietly. I asked what was wrong.

"I've lost my engagement ring," she said, angry at herself. "I've searched everywhere, but it's gone."

I told her not to worry: The ring had slipped down the bathroom-sink drain that morning, and a plumber could get it out easily.

"How do you know that, Shawn?" she asked. "You have no way of knowing where that ring is. You could be mistaken."

I told her I was very sure the ring was in the sink drain, and she should call a plumber immediately. But my mother wouldn't hear of it. Even in 1959, plumbers were expensive, and my psychic feelings were not enough to justify such an expenditure.

Later that afternoon, when my mother left to go to the store, I decided to take action on my own. In the house next to ours lived a retired plumber who occasionally did work for his neighbors at reduced rates. I walked over to see Mr. White.

When he came to the door, I got a cold chill the moment I saw him. Although he smiled broadly and was very friendly, I sensed something negative about him. I explained about the ring and the sink drain, and Mr. White came over with a few of his tools.

In the bathroom, he inserted a long snakelike wire down the drain and fished around for a few minutes. When he retracted the wire from the drain, my mother's engagement ring dangled from the end.

"There's our ring, little girl," said Mr. White jovially. I thanked him very much and asked him not to let my mother know of his visit. As he began to leave, I had a sudden urge to warn him of growing danger. I hesitated, unsure of myself. I didn't want to frighten him, but I kept having cold, dark feelings about his future. Finally I decided to say nothing. That afternoon, when my mother returned home, and I gave her the ring, she was so delighted that she took me out for an ice cream at a local soda shop.

A few weeks later Mr. White died of a heart attack. I felt guilty, wondering if I should have warned him. But then I learned that his heart condition had been serious for a number of years, and that he had, in fact, lived longer than the doctors had expected. His passing was quiet and peaceful.

Several times during my school year I foresaw a tragedy or misfortune. For a while, I believed that I was in some way responsible for these occurrences. In my young mind, the prediction and the event were so closely linked that the one seemed to cause the other. Only later did I realize I was never at fault.

The Bearer of Bad News

A young girl or boy has enough trouble just making sense of the world he or she lives in. ESP just makes it more confusing. I did not understand that, to some degree, the future already exists and can be seen by the gifted mind. So I began to dread my psychic experiences, fearing that each vision I had would bring pain or death to someone I loved. I thought God must have cursed me to bring harm to everyone I cared for. Everytime a vision came to me, I was filled with anxiety. I felt like King Midas, unable to touch anything without destroying it.

Then one day I had a frightening vision concerning my sister, Helene. At first, I just got a feeling that something bad might happen. It was not a clear vision of any specific event, but my fear sharpened it into a nightmare. I believed my sister would die in a terrible car crash—and I assumed it would be my fault. For days, like a prison guard, I watched my sister's comings and goings. Every time she left the house I struggled not to cry. At times I begged her to stay in and play music with me rather than go see her friends.

One afternoon that week, my sister planned a trip with her friend's family. The family drove to our house to pick her up. In my terrified imagination I believed this was the last time I would see my sister alive. As Helene left the house I began to cry and scream, pleading with her not to go. I wanted to mention my vision, but thought that merely uttering the words of doom would make the tragedy even more unavoidable. When Helene had departed, I ran to my room and wept, certain that my sister was gone forever—and that it was my fault. My mother came upstairs, but I was beyond comfort. In my mind, my terrible power of prediction had killed my only sister.

A few hours later, as I lay on my bed—having finally cried myself to sleep—my sister returned home. I heard her voice downstairs, telling my parents what fun she'd had that day.

I leapt from my bed and ran down the stairs. In the living room my sister stood, holding a helium-filled balloon, talking with my mother. I ran to her and hugged her, delighted that she had survived. "What was the accident like?" I asked. "Was anyone else hurt?" But she just laughed, probably thinking I was crazy.

It was a tremendous relief that my sister returned home safely that day, but it also caused me to reconsider my ideas about precognition. Obviously I was *not* causing things to happen, or my sister would have been harmed just as I had imagined. Also, I could have false predictions: My visions of the future might not *always* come true.

I had mixed feelings about these revelations. Of course I was glad to know that I was not causing tragedy but it took a little wind out of my sails to learn that I could be wrong. To this day I still have false visions, but I have learned how to adjust to failure. It seems to me that a responsible psychic is obligated to give all the information he or she can. If I foresee tragedy, I do not keep it to myself out of fear of being proven wrong. If a prediction will cause sorrow, I would be the first person to cheer if it proves false—but this does not prevent me from reporting as many of my feelings as the clients can handle. The most honest and fair approach is to tell them all I can, reminding them that I do not have God's itinerary for the future, and that many of my predictions may be false.

As time went on, the nature of my predictions began to change from childlike concerns like the location of lost toys, to adult concerns like death and tragedy—a change that seems to have coincided with my own growth. At each stage of my development, in fact, my visions have been related to my personal interests.

This gives strong support for the theory that ESP and precognition are actually *mental* functions, and not always messages from outside oneself. The content of a psychic's vision is greatly determined by his or her own thoughts and feelings.

There is another type of vision, however, which does indeed come from beyond one's own mind. For example, predictions of plane crashes or bombings come to me from an unknown, distant source. I certainly have no interest in any such activities, yet I did not have this kind of vision until I was grown and mature. While many precognitions will have little evident connection with me, I know that for some important reason they have been sent to me instead of to another psychic. That is, I doubt that a six-year-old child with psychic powers is likely to envision a mass murder!

Like most kids, I made it through elementary school—perhaps just barely, but I made it. The sixties were about to begin and soon the Beatles would be on *The Ed Sullivan Show.*

I was filled with longing for and anticipation of high school. Having a locker, enjoying free periods and study halls, These small changes were like blessings from heaven to me and my friends.

I began to sense that the world was not as I had thought. I heard my first rumors about the birds and the bees, and like most kids, found the whole idea preposterous. Like any young girl, I was an incurable romantic, and had dreamed for years about my first love. Of course, my dreams were different: Mine would come true!

By this time, my father had opened his own tool and die company, and the employee's worries and troubles had turned into an employer's responsibilities and pressures. While we were never wealthy, money had become less of a problem.

My sister and I were still playing music together, she on accordion and I on guitar, for local clubs and organizations. Helene was beginning to develop the same fears of psychic power that my mother and I had experienced. In a few years these fears—combined with her strong interest in religion—would lead her to abandon her powers and allow them to fade.

Perhaps this was just as well. Psychic powers can provide a lot of advantages, but Helene would not have relished the burden of horror and fear that my gift brought me. Believing I would find new friends in high school who would not know about my powers, I committed myself to keeping them a secret. Fortunately or otherwise, it did not work out that way.

4
Denial and Romance

As adolescence neared, I faced a terrible decision. Did I want to be like Annette Funicello or Doris Day? Try as I might, I just couldn't decide.

I was determined that my teen years would not be ruined by mysterious predictions and visions. I would put all that behind me, out of my mind. To the world I would be nothing more than Shawn Robbins, average kid, just like everyone else. There was nothing I wanted less during those years than psychic power.

But in the 1960's, just being average was difficult enough. These were times of great confusion and upheaval. My generation would soon rebel against everything our parents had taught us.

Slowly I was becoming aware of the day-to-day horrors that occur in our world. The Cuban missile crisis terrified my neighborhood. In school we would have air-raid drills, sitting on the hall floor with our heads between our knees.

In all, it was a terrible time to be a teenager. Adolescents have always been confused about themselves and the world, rebelling to some degree, and searching for answers to unfathomable questions. But during the sixties, the answers never seemed to come. Even the questions were hard to find.

High School

In 1960 new freedoms came fast and furious. Suddenly I was picking courses, making schedules, and having free periods during the day. At first it felt like vacation, for I had been accustomed to having most of my decisions made for me. I never liked the arrangement, but it certainly was easy. The pressure of choosing a curriculum for myself, considering college, pursuing extracurricular activities, even deciding what to wear—it was all confusing.

During those years, I grew further away from my parents, as every child does during adolescence. My parents resented my new freedom, fearing that I would grow up and leave them forever. I even lost some of the closeness I had always shared with my sister. She was several years older than I and our interests were no longer the same. I had more important things to worry about—like whether the Monkees were going to break up as a singing group!

And throughout these years the visions came, despite my effort to wish them away. Almost every day, I would have some precognition concerning the next day or the years to come, or I would suddenly find myself reading someone's mind. Whenever my powers announced themselves, I repressed them, refusing to pay any attention. Determined to be more popular in high school that I had been before, I tried to learn the secrets that only the popular girls seemed to know. (The most common "secret" was early physical development!) I wanted to be like everyone else—innocent, fun-loving, and naive. But my visions terrified me, especially when I could not make them go away. I began to fear that I would have a life filled with images of death and destruction, and still hoped that this fate could be avoided. I always wanted to advise my friends—to let them know which of their plans wouldn't work out, or tell them which romances would end in disappointment. But I had to stop myself, out of fear that others would discover my gift and ridicule me.

An Imaginary Romance

During that first year of high school, a girl named Mary was my closest friend and confidante. We shared so many things together! I told her more about myself than I had ever told anyone except my sister or my grandmother. Mary knew everything about me—except that I was psychic.

We were only fifteen, but our interests had already turned to romance, and Mary had developed an overpowering crush on Tom, one of the boys at school. At first Tom didn't even know Mary was alive. So the two of us planned ways to get his attention, arranging to be in places where he would notice her. After classes we'd stand behind the school, talking and waiting for Tom and the rest of the track team to come out for practice. During lunch we'd find a table in the cafeteria near where he sat with his friends. Eventually, when Tom began to talk to Mary, she was convinced that her first romantic experience would lead to eternal love. I was very happy for her, but sensed that Tom didn't seem to return her feelings. And whenever I spoke with him, I felt that he wasn't really interested in Mary.

Within a few days Mary was in seventh heaven, sure that Tom was about to ask her to go steady. I wanted to tell her that I had sensed negative feelings in him, but knew she might get angry if I did. (And I didn't want to tell her that the feelings I sensed usually came true!)

Soon Mary had convinced herself that she and Tom were dating. Behind her back the other kids at school laughed at her, thinking she was making a fool of herself. It hurt me to see my best friend treated this way.

Every time Mary talked about Tom, their imaginary relationship took on new dimensions. Soon she began to picture how handsome they would look together at the senior prom; eventually she was planning on marriage and children. A lifetime relationship existed in her mind—and Tom hadn't yet taken her on a date. Mary was just having a relatively minor schoolgirl's fantasy, and the problem would have worked itself out eventually. But at fifteen, I didn't want to see my best friend embarrassed and humiliated. I had doubts about Tom's true feelings for Mary, but if I was going to mention them to Mary, I had to be sure. Just this once, I decided I should use my psychic powers to help a friend. One day that week I managed to get Tom into conversation. I don't remember what we talked about, but it didn't matter—I just wanted to hear his voice and look into his eyes so I could get impressions from him.

As he talked, Tom's feelings also came through loud and clear. He was interested in Mary only as a friend. He had no desire to hurt her, but none to date her either. Reading his mind, I sensed that he was actually dating someone else—a girl I didn't know. I desperately wanted to tell Mary what I knew, but how would I explain? "Mary, I read Tom's mind and found out that he's dating someone else"? She'd never believe that; besides, I still wanted to conceal my psychic power.

One night when Mary came over to my house, we barricaded ourselves in my room and had a heavy session of girl talk. All Mary could think about, of course, was Tom. She went on and on about him—sure he would ask her out on a date any day now.

"I know he wants to ask me to go steady," Mary said. "He's just waiting for the right moment to ask me. He's very romantic, you know."

Tom was romantic, all right—but not about Mary.

"Mary, I . . . are you *sure* Tom likes you that much?"

"Course I'm sure. Why? What's the matter?"

"Well, it's just that if he *really* wanted to date you, I think he would have asked you by now."

"He's real shy, that's all."

"Mary," I said, searching for the right words, "I don't think Tom is ever going to ask you out. I think he's dating someone else, some girl we don't know."

"Who? How do you know?"

"I just . . . I just know, that's all."

"Did you see him with someone? Did someone tell you he's got another girl?"

"No . . ."

"Then *how* do you know?"

"I just know. I can tell."

Mary was very upset and confused, and I couldn't blame her. "I just don't get it," she sobbed. "Why are you doing this to me?"

"Mary, please . . ."

"Why are you making up stories to hurt me? I thought we were friends."

"We *are* best friends. I just don't want to see you get hurt."

"Then why are you trying to hurt me now? I bet you like Tom too, don't you?"

I tried to convince her I just wanted to protect her feelings and save her pain, but she wouldn't believe me. And I couldn't prove any of the things I said about Tom.

In a moment she had grabbed her coat and left. The next day at school she refused to talk to me. I knew how she felt, I just wished I could do something to make her understand the situation.

During that week Annie, one of the biggest brats in our class that year, told me I was smart to dump Mary as a friend. Mary was being ridiculous about Tom, she said, and everyone knew it except Mary. This cruel gossip and cattiness made me furious.

Proof at the School Dance

I had no date for the next Saturday night's school dance, and I tried to get Mary to go with me. But she wouldn't even let me talk to her. We each went to the dance alone. I stood to the side on the gymnasium floor and danced with just about everyone who asked me. Meanwhile, Mary waited near the door for Tom to arrive. Even though he hadn't asked her to the dance, she still believed he was in love with her.

Finally Mary saw Tom come through the door, and a great smile spread across her face, then she started moving toward him. Suddenly her entire world collapsed. Tom was with another girl. (Later I learned that her name was Cathy and that she went to a private school nearby.) Once again my psychic feelings had been correct, but they were of no help to Mary now. To hide her tears, she put her hand over her face and ran from the gymnasium.

I thought about chasing after her, but she didn't want to talk to me, especially now. On a night like this, anything I could say would sound like: "I told you so."

Suddenly Annie appeared behind me. "Boy!" she said, "Mary really made a jerk of herself this time. She'll never live this one down in a million years!"

Annie's insensitivity made me livid. I swung round and did something I've never done before or since. I hit Annie, right on the mouth. She fell on her fanny, bursting into tears like a two-year-old, and was I delighted! But that display of anger cost me ten demerits and two days of detention duty—picking up candy wrappers and empty cigarette packs from the school grounds. Of course, my parents were horrified, and spent the next week wondering if they had raised a criminal maniac!

Mary found out about my run-in with Annie, and she visited me during detention. Soon we were close friends again, and everyone forgot the incident—along with her infatuation with Tom.

But teenagers can change so quickly, virtually reversing personality traits within a few months. As time passed, Mary and I drifted apart. Our interests diverged and soon she and I spoke to one another only occasionally.

A New Problem With ESP

Among the many confusing problems of adolescence, sex is probably the most endlessly fascinating. At first the whispered rumors that circulate the school yard seem shocking and unimaginable. But in time, Mom or Dad sits the child down for a long discussion, which clarifies at least a few of the rumors.

As my body changed and developed I, like any child, had longed to understand all the secrets that had been kept hidden from me. I wanted to be an adult, and I wanted to fall in love.

Along with all my friends, I waited anxiously, searching for that special boy who would be just perfect for me. We would meet, fall instantly in love with each other, go steady for about seven years, then marry and have children. That's what I was hoping for.

But first of all, it seemed to take the boys a few years to catch up with us. While my girl friends and I fantasized about torrid love affairs with rock stars and movie idols, the boys still played baseball. They just didn't seem interested. But within a few years they had a change of heart. More and more, I would look to them at school and at weekend parties. During gym class and after school I would catch them looking at me and knew they were interested in me. I liked quite a few of these young men. And perhaps most of all, I liked the fact that they liked me. But my own attitudes and psychic abilities always held me back from my first case of puppy love.

I was determined that my first love would be my last—that the first boy I dated would become my eventual husband, so I had an exceptionally difficult time finding a suitable candidate. Whereas other girls might have imagined that a certain young fellow was the man of their dreams, my psychic powers didn't allow me any such flights of fancy. I *knew* that none of these young men would ever be right for me.

Even when one seemed interesting from a distance or in conversation, I would receive visions of his future—or mine— and foresee that he would never share my life. If love would not last, I was determined not to let it begin.

Romance is never simple, especially not when you're psychic, but I doubt now that this was the right attitude to take. In order to experience and enjoy love, a state of blissful optimism is crucial. The possibility of breaking up must be unthinkable—at least in the beginning. For love to flourish, one must concentrate only on the beautiful possibilities ahead.

Does he like me? Will he ask me to marry him? When you're in love, these are the important questions, reflecting hope, faith, and confidence in the future.

But I could not ask any such questions—because I already knew the answers! And I couldn't start a relationship that I already saw doomed. And so although I dated and socialized, I never had a big high-school romance. Naturally I was disappointed, but I knew ahead of time that happiness would not come yet.

So through my high-school years, my resolution to accept a sequestered, lonely life grew even stronger. Soon I would fall completely into a day-to-day pattern of solitude and self-absorption. For me, high school was losing a lot of its initial charm. After the novelty wore off, changing classes and going out for walks during study hall became just another familiar routine.

Kids my age began to divide into different groups and cliques. Some were jocks—always clean-cut, cheerleader types, idolizing sports heroes, and double-dating at the movies. Others became rebels, hippies-to-be, so to speak. They let their hair grow long, wore dirty clothes, despised sports and loved the Rolling Stones. Naturally I was shocked to hear rumors about kids smoking pot and experimenting with sex.

Some of my classmates were eggheads, avoiding social functions, wearing terribly unfashionable clothes, and spending their spare time forming organizations like the Social Studies Club. And a few kids who didn't belong to any group at all just kept to themselves, hiding their feelings and looking painfully lonely.

I didn't know which of these groups I belonged in. I experimented with all of them—except the eggheads' group, of course.

I felt very alone during that first year or so of high school. And as hard as I tried to fit in, I still remained isolated. My visions continued to occur more and more often. I prayed to God to make them go away, to let me be normal like everyone else, but my prayers were not answered. In my visions I saw myself in the years to come, still alone and separated from the rest of the world by my powers which I thought of as a curse.

I was about to turn sixteen, but life tasted bitter. I could not deny my psychic nature, and my visions and feelings pursued me with dogged determination. I was forced to realize I would never be like everyone else. My own interests and concerns would always take second place to the images of other people's tragedies. And there was nothing I could do about it.

After my friendship with Mary ended, I turned more and more to my family, passing long afternoons in my room. During those years, I became an avid reader of nonfiction, particularly biographies of famous people, and every biographical novel I could find. Did I simply enjoy reading biographies or could I somehow have known that one day I would deal with the rich and famous and achieve some fame myself?

A Walk Too Far

Some days I took my squash racket out to the park and stood in front of the handball court, playing squash with myself.

Often I went for long walks around our section of Queens, already showing signs of being the night person I am today. I could think more clearly after sundown, and after dark I noticed a definite increase in psychic phenomena. One evening when I felt particularly alone, I covered blocks and blocks, not giving much thought to my distance from home.

Beside a small park, I suddenly felt as though the temperature had dropped ten degrees in as many seconds. I stopped, believing that perhaps a vision was about to come to me. But all I felt was that uncomfortable chill and a sense that something was not right. I turned to look into the blackness of the trees in the park, but saw nothing except the darkness.

Suddenly I heard the clink of a beer bottle falling to the ground. At that instant, my feeling of isolation disappeared. Someone was watching me; danger was imminent. Realizing how far from home I was, I turned, walking quickly back the way I'd come. I didn't turn to look, but I could feel them behind me, following. In my mind I saw four young men, eighteen or nineteen. From the garbled messages I was receiving, I could guess without any trouble that they were drunk. I increased my pace, hoping to reach a more brightly lit street or an open store or shop. But the blocks ahead offered no refuge.

I tried to focus on these men's thoughts. It was hard to get a clear image, but for perhaps the first time in my life, I feared for my own safety.

I kept walking faster and faster. My speed was involuntary, almost automatic. But my pursuers drew closer and closer. Panic was beginning to overwhelm me. I wanted to run, but knew they would pounce on me at the first sign of flight.

Suddenly I felt my mother's presence. I couldn't clear my mind enough to receive her message, but I knew that she was trying to help me.

Then this message grew very strong, filling me with calm and confidence. I halted in my attempt to escape and spun around to face my pursuers.

When I turned, the men leaped out of sight behind some hedges. Although I couldn't see them, I knew that my impression that there were four of them had been correct. I stood stock-still, looking into the bushes where they were hiding, trying desperately to focus in on their thoughts — and miraculously, I succeeded. Getting a clear impression that one of them was named Steve, I decided to take action.

"Steve!" I shouted. "Get out of here and leave me alone, or I'll tell your dad!"

A second's silence, then I heard the men whispering in the darkness.

"How did you know his name?" one of them asked. "Do we know you?" It now seemed that *they* were the frightened ones.

A second name came into my mind. "Of course you know me, Jack. Now leave me alone!"

With that, I simply turned and continued toward home. I didn't know whether my attempt to frighten them would backfire. They might now want to eliminate a potential "witness." I walked as quickly as I could without revealing my terror, and in a block or two I knew they were no longer following me.

I was still several blocks away from home when my father's car came down the street. He stopped by the curb and I got in, relieved to see him.

"Is something wrong?" he asked. It seems my mother had been suddenly overcome with fear for me. Sensing I was in danger, she sent my father out in the car to find me. Her fear had come from me, of course, and her presence and strength had come to me in telepathic response.

I put an immediate stop to these distant journeys by night. My psychic powers had been very effective, but I had no intention of pressing my luck!

5
A Visit to Maria

As I grew from young adolescence to adulthood, I was constantly being shaped and molded by my environment and by the people around me. In my family, extraordinary powers were commonplace, and were honed and sharpened every single day. But at the same time my mother's fears and uncertainties had caused me many anxieties and doubts about this special path of life that lay before me.

During those years, when I drifted into isolation and turned in on myself, searching and exploring my heart, testing and defining my abilities, alternately denying and enjoying my gift, I desperately needed someone who could understand and encourage me.

True, I read every book I could find on the topic of psychic phenomena. And these books did bring me comfort that I was not alone. Out there in this world were others like myself, people who had the same powers but who did not need to deny or suppress them. But a book cannot listen to your troubles or console you when you feel alone or frightened.

One night I was sitting alone in my room in our house in Queens, poring over another volume about Edgar Cayce, perhaps the greatest psychic who ever lived. As I sat on my bed, surrounded by the symbols of my youth—my aging guitar, dolls, and posters—I found myself daydreaming about my future, imagining myself as a famous psychic like Cayce, with my amazing achievements destroying the doubts of nonbelievers.

Suddenly my dream disappeared, and I was overwhelmed with feelings of insecurity. How could I ever become a professional psychic? Did I want to lead a life of nonconformity, rejected and shunned by normal society?

For several years I had been trying to do all I could to deny my powers—without success—but now I renewed my commitment to be as normal as possible . . . even if it meant a lifetime of secrecy, of keeping my visions and predictions to myself. But still, even though I was convinced that this was my only choice, something was nagging at my heart. A battle was raging within me—how could I ever completely hide my powers? And didn't I have an obligation to use my gift for good, to help my fellow human beings? Perhaps more than ever before, I needed someone to talk to—not my mother or my friends at school, but someone outside of my life who could give me a little objective advice.

Without knowing why, I got up from my bed. I walked out into the dark hallway, down the staircase, and headed directly for the kitchen. With almost no thoughts in my mind, no special purpose leading me onward, I reached up to a shelf in the kitchen and got down the phone book. I gazed down at the page to which I had opened, and among the dozens of names and phone numbers, I saw one name standing, almost shining: Maria Bliekers. I did not need to write down her number, for it had instantly been stamped on my consciousness

I opened the door that led from the kitchen to the basement. Now almost in a trance, without even turning on the light I walked down the old steps into the damp cellar. Normally I was terrified of a dark cellar, but this time, shining ahead of me was a strange, yellow light that led to my father's workshop. The workshop was filled with the pieces of another gadget my father was repairing. To avoid tripping on them, I did not even need to look down. Some force guided my feet over the pieces of metal and wood.

My father had put in a telephone extension so he would not have to run upstairs whenever the phone rang in the kitchen.

In complete darkness, without even knowing what my hands were doing, I dialed the number I had seen upstairs. At the other end, the phone rang once—not even a full ring. And suddenly there was a soothing, gentle, woman's voice on the line, answering. I did not speak, I only listened.

"Hello, Shawn, she said. "I am glad you have called me. I want to tell you that everything is going to be all right, and I would like to invite you to come see me soon. I am looking forward to your visit very much. Come whenever you can, and we can have a nice talk. And for now, please do not be worried. I tell you truly, everything will work out just fine."

Still without having said a word, I hung up the receiver, turned and walked back up to the kitchen, and then returned to my room. As I lay on my bed, her words repeated themselves over and over in my mind like a lullaby easing me into sleep. I closed my eyes, and dreamed of Maria Bliekers.

The next day, I decided to play hooky. I headed away from school, went down into the subway, and traveled into Manhattan.

For the first time, I was traveling alone into the city. I had no idea what subway or bus lines I would need to take, and yet something guided me. I found myself getting off one train, onto another, and continuing my journey, unsure where it would lead me.

But as the train pulled into one stop, I suddenly knew that I was near my destination. I got off the subway and walked up to the city street.

Without even looking around, I headed immediately north for a few blocks, passing fashionable boutiques, restaurants, and antique shops.

When I came to a small apartment house, I knew that I had reached my goal. In the tiled foyer I looked at the panel of buzzers, apartment numbers, and names. Among them was M. Bliekers.

I reached out to push the button to tell her that someone was here to visit her. But before I touched it, the door lock opened electronically from within—she had somehow known of my arrival, and had buzzed me in.

After two flights of stairs an opened door stood before me. I could not see inside the apartment, and no one awaited me at the door. Yet I entered without fear or question.

As I crossed the threshold my trancelike state came to an end. Suddenly, before I could even look around, I knew where I was.

Instead of some kind of gypsy tent filled with tapestry and beads and amulets, the apartment was simple and neat, filled with antiques and framed needlepoint on the walls. The living room was painted a shade of plum that was at once exciting and soothing. Against one wall was a lovely couch, and on it sat Maria Bliekers.

"Hello, Shawn! I am so glad that you came today. Won't you sit down?" Her voice rang with the same musical quality I had heard on the phone the night before.

I sat down beside her silently. She smiled, and her eyes—those of a kind and loving woman—shone with a brillance and a depth I had never seen before.

"You are troubled, Shawn, by your powers. You do not understand why you have been chosen for this task in life, and I know just how you feel. You see, *I* have been chosen to help you. From this day on, our lives will be intertwined, my dear. What happens to you, what troubles you, will also concern me. I will always be here to help, should you need me. And one day, when you no longer need my guidance, I shall be gone.

"Right now, I must tell you two things. The first concerns your gift. Shawn, you need not agonize yet about your future. There is no pressure on you to become a professional psychic. You are still a young girl. What you must do is simply live your life as it comes. Follow your interest in music, for it will lead you toward your true path in life. And do not suppress your predictions. Accept them, acknowledge them—and share them with those you love."

I listened more carefully to her words than I had ever listened to my teachers in school.

"In time," she continued, "your path will be revealed to you. When finally there is no way you can escape it, your power will begin to control your destiny. But this, my child, is all many years ahead. It cannot be rushed—and you need not be afraid of it."

As she spoke, I felt at ease, comforted by her words, as though a great cloud was lifting from my heart. Like my grandmother years before, Maria Blieker knew my thoughts, and understood what was troubling me.

A Prayer

"The second thing I must tell you is a simple prayer that I want you to repeat twice a day, or whenever you feel the need. This is the prayer . . ." Her eyes closed slowly, her head tilted back, and she began to chant: "With the infinite good that is within me, I pray to the infinite good within you, dear God. And with the infinite good that is within you, dear God, please pray for the infinite good within me."

I did not need to ask her to repeat those words or write them down. I would never forget them.

"Now," she asked lovingly, "do you have any questions or problems that we can talk about?"

It was like being shocked out of a deep sleep. All the thoughts that had been plaguing me for years were suddenly swept from my mind. I paused a moment, searching for something to say, but then simply shook my head.

"Very good. Then I recommend that you get back to school as soon as you can. And remember, say your prayer, and call me any time you want to—any time at all."

With that, I said simply, "Thank you," and left her apartment.

In the weeks and months to come, I would repeat that simple prayer two, three, even five times a day, and each time I felt better, more secure, more loved. From time to time I would call Maria about a certain problem. Each time I called, she would anticipate my questions before I asked them and, in simple words, she would comfort me and give me strength. Although we spoke only occasionally, I felt her presence around me every minute of each day. Without question, she was the closest friend I had.

Turning to Music

Despite all the excitement and the new ideas of the age of Aquarius, I didn't really need to experiment with drugs or communal living. I didn't need to become a hippie in order to be unconventional.

Within a year or so of my meeting Maria, I decided not to finish high school. Naturally this drove my parents wild with anger and disappointment (and today, it's a decision that I very much regret). But my isolation had grown so total that I could never imagine going to college, holding a regular job, or gaining any other possible benefit from a high-school diploma. So I decided to forego higher education and pursue music, the only other interest that had ever appealed to me.

When I called Maria and told her about my decision to quit school (fully expecting her to be as disappointed and upset as my parents were) she simply told me to do what I felt was right, and keep saying the prayer she had taught me. As I hung up the phone, I began to repeat the words in my mind: "With the infinite good that is within me, I pray to the infinite good within you, dear God . . ."

Through contacts I had made while performing with my sister, I got an audition for an all-women's band that was forming to play pop and cocktail music—familiar material to me—and had no trouble getting into the group as their electric bass player.

Our band toured the country for several years. We played in just about every city, town, and backwoods club imaginable. We traveled almost constantly, no sooner settling into one town than we left it for another. Our accommodations were usually at very simple, inexpensive little hotels that would make a Holiday Inn look like a jet-set resort!

For a few years I lived and breathed music, far too busy to spend much time wondering about my gift. And yet I could not keep my visions from coming, or myself from giving unsolicited advice. So I was never quite sure what my fellow musicians thought of me. And at the same time, my visions came with more power and fury than ever before; some too powerful to be suppressed.

Again, Visions of Danger

One day, when the band was aboard a bus to the airport, I had a frightening sense of danger for myself and the others.

Something told me that the small jet plane waiting for us was unsafe. Shutting my eyes, I saw myself and my friends high up in the clouds, terrified to learn that our plane could not land—or would soon crash to earth. The vision was vague, so that I could not be certain what was wrong with the plane, or when the danger would occur. I tried to tell the others that our trip would not go smoothly, but—naturally—they teased me about my prediction, saying that I was just nervous, or upset about something else. At this point, I, myself, even found it difficult to put much faith in my vision. I had tried to deny it for so long that I had come to doubt it. So I went along with their joking, and—against my better judgment—boarded the plane.

After the first few hours of flight, the pilot announced that one of the engines had developed mechanical trouble. We were lucky enough to land safely at a nearby small-town airport.

While maintenance people checked the plane over, we spent the night in a dreary waiting area. Some of us tried to sleep in our chairs. As the sun started to creep up toward the horizon, a representative of the airline came to tell us that the plane had been repaired and that we would be able to take off soon. My friends, anxious to reach our destination and find a hotel bed to sleep in, were all delighted by this news. But I was still troubled. Something told me that our plane was yet unsafe, and that our lives would be endangered if we left the ground.

After a few more hours of flight—hours that saw me sitting nervously, staring out the windows at the morning sky—the pilot's voice came over the intercom again, reporting further engine trouble. For the second time in our trip, we would have to land short of our destination. All the other musicians were disgusted at the airline's apparent incompetence in getting us where we wanted to go. But I was simply delighted to hear that we would soon land—for I sensed that any further travel would bring us closer not to our next gig, but to our deaths.

This time the engine trouble could not be corrected even after several hours of work. The plane was grounded, and we continued on our way in a second jet.

After this, the band began to take my predictions more seriously. Often they would come to me for personal advice about their careers, their love lives, or about health problems. And yet, *I* still had not realized that my destiny lay with my gift; that my career as a musician would soon be over.

6

Romance and a New Career

Though my desire for love and romance continued to grow as I grew older, I knew there was still no point in seeking them. I could see far enough into my own future to know I would not find a love partner.

The person I would love would have to be a very special person. But in addition to being someone I could enjoy being with, he would almost certainly have to be psychic—or at least have a strong belief and interest in psychic phenomena. Otherwise there would be just too many aspects of my life he would never be able to share; too many feelings and fears and joys that we would never experience together.

Mr. Right?

When I was twenty-one, I was still pursing my musical career, giving private readings to friends and fellow musicians.

One night a man named Jack, who had been listening to our band, introduced himself to me when our session was over. He fit almost exactly my image of what a handsome man should look like. He was tall, a little over six feet, his eyes a strong and piercing blue, like the color of the sky just before dawn breaks. His clean, rugged features gave him a look of experience and wisdom. His body was lean, like that of a man who works hard for his living.

When he spoke, I got positive but confused feelings about him. I could tell at once from his eyes that he was interested in me, and I also felt that his attraction was to me as a total person. But this was as far as my vision was able to probe. As much as I listened to his voice, as hard as I tried to see into his mind, it was as though some great leaden wall my powers could not penetrate was shielding his inner thoughts and feeling.

That first night, this handsome, fascinating man took me out for coffee at a local diner. We sat in an old-fashioned leather booth, and I listened to him talk about his life, his work, and his dreams.

Jack was a businessman in charge of inventory for a local manufacturing company. His job consisted largely of bookkeeping—knowing what items were sitting in the warehouse, ordering supplies, shipping products to client companies and affiliates. His work paid well and allowed him to live comfortably, he said, but Jack had always harbored a dream of working outdoors, perhaps in conservation, and had considered studying forestry in college. However, pressures from his family had led him to follow the more secure path of a business career.

Now thirty years old, he was beginning to realize that he might never attain his goal of working in the wild. I tried to concentrate my powers on him and this career question, just as I would when giving a personal reading today. But I was unable to recieve any visions of what lay in store for Jack. Soon he asked me about my music. I told him that I enjoyed a musician's life, but that I was also psychic, and that many of my friends were urging me to utilize my powers full time.

Jack was more than a little surprised to hear this. He leaned back in the booth slowly, as if the word *psychic* had pushed him gently away. He smiled half convincingly and his face registered momentary confusion, as if he were struggling to find something appropriate to say.

"That's very unusual," he said, and went on to tell me that the field of psychic phenomena, although rather new to him, seemed very interesting. He'd read several articles and seen televised reports on the subject. He believed in psychic powers and would like to know more.

After our third cup of coffee, he walked me back through the darkened streets to the little hotel where the band members were staying. As we approached the hotel door, I tried to look into Jack's mind, wondering if he intended to kiss me or invite himself in—or even just ask to see me again. But I could still get no impressions of his thoughts.

When he *did* ask if he might kiss me good night, I said yes. It was a short, sweet kiss, yet it sent waves of emotion through me. You see, even the smallest physical contact between people heightens our intuitive and subconscious powers. And for a psychic like myself, a kiss can send bright, colorful patterns showering through the mind and soul.

But even in this supersensitive moment, I found to my annoyance that I still could not get any psychic feelings about Jack. This mental block was rare for me—and especially confusing when it happened with someone I already felt close to. Before he left that night, we agreed to meet the next day.

I went up to my small but pleasant hotel room, and sat on the edge of my bed. I looked around at the small framed pictures of ships and trees and rivers on the hotel walls. The three cups of coffee I'd drunk were making my nervous system jumpy, and for hours I sat up thinking about Jack and wondering why I could not read his mind.

Over the next few days, we went to dinner several times and saw a few movies, spending many hours together. But mostly we just walked and talked, sometimes at my hotel or at his apartment. The more I spoke with Jack and learned about him, the more I felt that I might be falling in love with him—but I still could not get into his mind!

This nagging fact should have been an obvious indication to me that we would never be right for each other. But—probably because I was lonely—I decided to ignore my intuition. Finally, after so many years of meeting young, attractive men and *knowing* we would never be together, I had met a man who interested me—and without the burden of foreseeing a breakup, without the saddening awareness I had always had of the future, I was free to be optimistic, free to fall in love.

Finally the day came when our band had finished its bookings in town, and we prepared to move on. I was filled with questions and doubts—should I stay and pursue my relationship with Jack? Or leave and see how strongly my emotions would pull me back to him? If I did leave now, would he soon forget me and find someone else?

I wanted him, and yet I was very unsure of my own feelings. After twenty-one years of always knowing whether I was doing the right thing, of letting my psychic gift show me the right thing to do, I was on my own now, thrown into the guessing game that nongifted people are forced to play every day. This was something new for me, something I was terribly insecure about. I didn't know what to do.

When you first fall in love, of course, you have no guarantee of happiness, no signed document assuring you that you will be completely happy. You have to judge your feelings and follow your intuition, trusting that things will work out as you hope they will. But I had grown so used to knowing things in advance—with certainty—that this sudden failure of my powers was nearly devastating. I simply did not know which way to turn.

This "Psychic Stuff"

Then came what may have been a psychic vision, or just the ordinary feeling anyone might have about someone they care about. I was overwhelmed by a feeling that Jack should quit his job in business and pursue his dream of working in the wild. Unless he gave his real goal in life one good try before giving up on it, I had a very strong feeling that he would not be happy. So that night I decided to tell Jack about my vision of his future.

That evening he picked me up at the hotel and we walked to a little neighborhood Chinese restaurant. As we sat at a table for two, looking over our menus and sipping tea, I could tell that Jack felt as confused and despondent as I did about my inevitable departure. For a while we tried to make small talk, discussing the good times we'd had in the last few days. We talked about the future, and the boundless possibilities it held for us. Then Jack brought up the subject of our relationship.

I stopped him before he could say anything that might change my mind about him. At that moment I liked him very much. In fact, I thought I loved him. But my lack of insight into his mind still confused me so that I dreaded the idea of his even asking me to stay behind when the band headed on.

This tense moment seemed like a good time to tell Jack about my feeling concerning his career. "Something tells me," I said, "that you should quit your present job right away and pursue your forestry work. I can't say for sure if you'll be successful, but I know you won't be satisfied with your life if you don't at least give this a try."

At first Jack took my suggestion lightly. He was so trapped in his business career that he couldn't even imagine returning to school to study forestry.

"But," I told him, "it is absolutely necessary for you to take the risk. And with my psychic gift, I'm almost always right about things like this."

Then I understood why I had not been able to read Jack's mind!

He put down his cup of tea, paused anxiously for a moment, and then began to speak. He said that although he liked me very much, he couldn't see placing very much emphasis on this "psychic stuff," as he called it. And he certainly wasn't about to quit a high-paying job just because some young woman had had a vision of his working in the woods.

At this instant I knew that Jack and I would never be right for each other. My own desire *not* to see what was hidden in his heart had prevented me from seeing into his thoughts. Wanting to fall in love with Jack, I had stopped my own powers from showing me his true feelings.

The rest of the evening was uncomfortable, to say the least. We finished our meal with barely a word exchanged between us. He walked me back to the little hotel, but this time there was no good-night kiss. I knew I would never see Jack again. Although it was a sad time for me, what had happened was for the best. For me to have stayed behind with Jack, or to have let myself fall in love with him, would have been truly disastrous. Sooner or later I would have learned how he truly felt about my gift, and the pain would have been far greater than the disappointment of that last night with him.

For many years I continued without falling in love. And I again accepted the idea that there would be no man in my life. I was not completely content with this, perhaps, but I became used to it.

Traveling the country with the band, at times I felt close to the other musicians I worked and lived with. Other times, I felt more alone and isolated than ever before. Living in strange hotels in strange little towns, we performed at night and rarely saw the daylight. . .eating in all-night diners, packing and unpacking suitcases every few days. . .traveling by bus, train, and plane to another hotel in another little town somewhere.

And still, my prayer brought me back in spirit to Maria's apartment and the warmth and love I felt there. Even while the band was performing, in my mind I would be hundreds of miles away, repeating my prayer silently and thoughtfully.

I began to accept my gift more and more, as Maria had suggested I would. When a prediction came to me, I would listen closely to it. And if the prediction affected the life of someone around me, I would share it. And soon, I found my powers growing stronger each day. More and more, I could direct my visions to a certain topic, or to specific people.

Maria and I began to correspond. At least once every few days I would sit down and write a letter to her. And as we left each town, I would leave forwarding addresses to ensure that her letters would eventually reach me.

Through these letters my mentor told me stories of her own psychic career, describing setbacks, depressions, and triumphs she had experienced. I could see my own experience reflected in hers: At some point in her life, she had been just like me—uncertain and confused, but developing and growing more powerful.

Often she would recommend books on psychic phenomena, which always provided me with direct answers to questions that were troubling me. It was as though Maria knew my every thought and feeling, and could tell just what kind of answers I needed. But even when she was not teaching me all the amazing things she knew, her friendship alone was guiding me. Just hearing her voice from time to time on the phone was a learning experience.

Leaving the Band

After many months—and more concerts than I can count—I began to feel that a musical life-style was not for me. Making music no longer fulfilled the creative urge in my heart. I sensed that another path of creativity would bring me greater rewards. And with each passing day, I felt that my predictions were more fulfilling than my performances.

Still many months away from deciding to become a professional psychic, I decided to leave the group and return to New York. I called Maria long-distance one night to consult with her about this, but before I even told her what I was considering, or why I had called, she gave me her advice: "Come back to New York, Shawn. There will be a job with a large corporation waiting for you. It won't last very long, but it will lead you toward your ultimate goal."

By this time, I knew not even to question Maria's advice. I left the band and returned home.

As always, she was absolutely right. I did get a job with a big corporation, and the job did involve using my psychic powers.

7

The Corporate Clairvoyant

You may have heard that many corporations hire psychics to do some very sophisticated spying. And certain governments—notably Soviet Russia—are attempting to harness the mysterious powers of psychic energy.

Frankly, I am not at liberty to reveal any of the work that I have done for the United States government. (My work with the Chicago and New York police departments is a matter of record—and is discussed later in this book.)

But as for corporate spying, I have indeed had some adventures. About five years ago . . .

"Edward Kohn" calls . . .

It was a gray Tuesday morning in February when I received a curious—but not totally unexpected—telephone call.

In a deep, efficient voice the caller identified himself as Edward Kohn, pronouncing the name with such rehearsed nonchalance that I knew it must be an invention and not his real name. (For reasons of pride or privacy, many people hide behind a pseudonym when they first consult a psychic.)

The caller mentioned the name of a wealthy Manhattan builder who had, he said, recommended me. Without wasting any words, he suggested that we meet for an informal reading at the Café des Artistes, an attractive French restaurant not far from my apartment.

When I arrived ten minutes late for our appointment, the expensively dressed "Mr. Kohn" was already seated at a table near the window.

From the look of appraisal his dark eyes gave me, it was clear that he did not have just an ordinary reading in mind. As I was soon to discover, he was looking for a fortune-teller, in the most literal sense of the word.

I ordered a light salad, and listened with amusement as "Mr. Kohn" created a fictional account of himself that was as transparent as the crystal glasses on our table. In a confidential tone, he told me about his law career, about his pregnant girl friend. . . .

Soon I lost interest, and began to stare out the window at the street. Finally I could listen no more, and I spoke for the first time in ten minutes.

"This story is pure baloney," I said. "Your problem isn't a pregnant girl friend, it's your pregnant imagination!"

He looked up in surprise.

"You're a more or less happily married businessman," I continued. "*Not* a lawyer—probably an executive in a fashion house or cosmetics corporation. Now that you've administered your little test, let's discuss business, Mr.— Mr.— Wise."

"John West," he softly corrected me. (Name has been changed.)

I admit, what I had told him about himself mostly was good detective work. He'd taken off his wedding band, but the skin where it should have been was pale and silvery. I could tell he wasn't a lawyer, because he didn't talk in the abstract, roundabout way lawyers use. The cosmetics industry was an educated guess, based on the fact that his hair had been styled and on his liberal use of cologne. (I also knew that the Café des Artistes is a favorite with fashion and cosmetics executives.) And since he didn't want to talk about himself and didn't make a pass at me, I knew he must have business on his mind.

As for his name, his briefcase had given me the initials J.W. But the rest seemed to come to me from somewhere deep and far back in my brain—like an old memory. "Wise" had not been a direct hit, but it was close enough to "West" to get me hired.

I Go to Work

"John West" as he finally admitted, was vice-president of XYZ, one of the nation's largest corporations. After some astute questions about the nature of my gift, and some precautionary digging into my background, he offered me a job as the company's first corporate psychic.

One of the conditions of my employment was that the nature of my work remain an absolute secret. Only a few top people in the company, and the president, were to know who I was and why I was hired. (For reasons that will become clear later, I no longer feel bound to respect this agreement.)

The shareholders, West complained, would never understand why the company needed a professional psychic on the payroll. He said he knew of numerous Fortune 500 firms that employed psychics as consultants on a wide range of matters—but none would publicly admit to this practice "for fear of embarrassment." As a cover, I was to receive the elegantly imprecise title of "special marketing consultant."

What does a corporate psychic do? To answer this question, a little background on the idiosyncrasies of the cosmetic industry is necessary.

In 1972, when I first went to work, there were over a dozen major cosmetic companies in the country, each vying for a multi-million-dollar market in shampoos, toothpastes, lipsticks, soaps, eyeliners, and denture adhesives. Few businesses are as keenly competitive; few depend so entirely on advertising, promotion, and sexy packaging. And few businesses are as obsessed with "product intelligence"—a euphemism for spying on the competition and stealing their ideas. Consequently, cosmetics executives will try almost anything to get the edge—even a move as unorthodox and "visionary" as hiring a professional psychic.

It was my job to try to predict how the general public would respond to new products and new advertising campaigns.

Whenever I was needed, I would receive a phone call from John West, who would invite me to come for a day of consultation.

Usually when I arrived, I would be ushered into a large conference room, where I would take a seat in a Mies van der Rohe chair drawn up at a large oak conference table.

I didn't bring along a crystal ball in an attaché case—since I owned neither a crystal ball nor an attaché case! And I didn't insist on flickering candlelight.

It wasn't necessary to mystify the proceedings. When psychics resort to Hollywood hocus-pocus and all the trappings of the occult, they are usually trying to live up to their clients' expectations that they are capable of magic. Subdued lighting may aid concentration, but the rest is just so much flummery. These $75,000-a-year executives didn't want a séance—they wanted results.

Looking for all the world like a graduate of Wharton or Harvard, I would sit there and listen patiently while John West and one or two marketing specialists would describe the product and the market they were trying to reach. Then I would retire to another room to collect my impressions.

Except for the hours I had spent working as a typist, I had no business experience to fall back on. When my impressions were correct—and they were right a phenomenal percentage of the time—clairvoyance was the only possible explanation.

One of my first assignments was to project sales figures for a roll-on deodorant several months in advance. I had to rely entirely on my psychic gift, for I wasn't even given previous sales figures to go by. Almost instantly a number came to mind. To me, this number had no significance, of course, but it had just the right feel. I could see it plainly in my mind's eye, like an event in a dream. I think my employers were impressed by the assurance with which I spoke— and perhaps a little surprised that the figure I had come up with was even in the ball park.

As it turned out, this first prediction was one of the most accurate I ever made. My forecast was correct within a margin of a few hundred dollars, while their own economists, using sophisticated computer projections, had *under*estimated sales by more that eight thousand dollars!

After that, some of the marketing executives began to treat me with an almost superstitious awe. On their coffee breaks they would come to me privately and ask for advice on all sorts of personal matters. The president of the company, also suspended his skepticism and seemed to be entirely won over. He even made confidential company material available to me at my request. Such information isn't always essential to successful prophecy, but I have found that it helps to know as much as possible about the subject of my predictions. Like an inventor, I try to master all the facts before drawing forth an inspiration.

Indeed, there are many similarities between prophecy and invention. Sometimes I feel like Archimedes, lounging lazily in his bathtub and thinking of nothing in particular. Then something clicks. From out of nowhere a thought takes form, and seems so clear, so urgent, so obviously true, that it cannot be denied. According to legend, when the method for determining the purity of gold occurred to Archimedes, he was so exultant that he jumped up from his tub and shouted, "Eureka!" When I have an extrasensory experience, I feel a kind of giddy excitement and like that Greek scientist, I want to shout, "I've got it!"

"Don't Get On That Plane!"

Unfortunately, prophecy isn't always accompanied by a feeling of elation.

About two months after I went to work, I woke up feeling sick and queasy. For a moment I thought I was coming down with the flu. Then I recognized the feeling as an *emotional* response—a sensation I'd had before but couldn't place.

At about nine-thirty that morning John West called to tell me not to come to the office that day because a number of marketing executives were flying out to Denver for an important meeting. Only then did I recognize the feeling that had been nagging at me all morning.

It was the same paralyzing fear I used to have every time I went up in an airplane—a dread that it took me years to conquer.

"John" I asked, "are you going to be on that flight?"

"Sure," he laughed, "I love to travel."

When I put down the receiver, the sickness was more intense than ever. I couldn't stop thinking about it. Half an hour later I called him back.

"Don't get on that plane," I warned him. "Don't let *anyone* get on that plane!"

I must have sounded a little hysterical, and John tried to calm me down over the phone with some amateur psychology. Then he quoted the familiar statistics that claim air travel is safer than driving to the corner drugstore, smoking a cigarette, or taking a shower. "I promise not to shower the whole time I'm in Denver," he quipped.

"Don't be patronizing," I shot back. And then I saw it—literally. As clearly as if I were reading it off the fuselage, I saw the serial number on the plane: 297031. At the same time, I "knew" the pilot's name: Dan Rivers. And I knew if that plane ever got off the ground something terrible would happen.

I explained all this as rationally as I could. But John was not persuaded.

"I happen to know the pilot's name is Bradley," he said firmly. "It's a company plane, and I've flown with him a hundred times before."

I tried to warn him every way I could, to talk him out of making the trip. By the time he got off the line, I was in tears.

It took a few minutes for me to regain control of myself. Then I dialed the president's number. Chances were he wouldn't listen; chances were I'd lose my job. But I had to try.

When I finally got through to the president's office, his secretary told me that he and his wife were already on their way to the Westchester Airport.

At ten-thirty, I received John's call from the airport. Now it was *his* turn to be hysterical—the serial number I had given him was an exact hit, except that two of the digits were out of order!

Taking a deep breath, he said, "Shawn, I want you to know that Bradley, the regular pilot, called in sick this morning. The man assigned to take his place is Dan Rivers."

There was a long pause. Finally he said, "Can you come up here right away?"

Not waiting for the elevator, I ran down the stairs of my apartment building and flagged down the first cab I saw. It was a fifty-minute ride to the Westchester Airport.

I arrived to find the executives crowded into the tiny terminal. They were furious, but their wives were terrified. Apparently one of the women had had the same premonition of disaster that I had. By the expressions on their faces I could tell that *they* never would be convinced to get on that flight.

The president insisted that I go over the plane —a Rolls Royce jet, as I recall—inch by inch with the mechanics, who suspected that West was crazy for postponing the take-off. But they were absolutely certain that I was a raving lunatic! For some reason, I asked them about the condition of the left engine.

The chief mechanic arched his brows in surprise. "There *was* a problem with the pump," he conceded, "but we fixed that a couple of days ago. It's one hundred percent okay now."

The more I thought about it, the stronger my doubts became. By this time a dark cloud had moved silently over the airport, and it had started to rain. The president looked with evident relief at the tongues of lightning on the horizon. Here was the excuse he had been looking for, a way to save face.

Complaining bitterly about all the time I had wasted and all the fuss I had caused, the president cancelled the flight on the grounds that "the weather's gotten too rough to take a small jet now." Then he hired a limousine, shuttled the whole group over to LaGuardia Airport, and flew to Denver on a regularly scheduled flight.

Two days later West telephoned to tell me that the mechanics had discovered that the replacement pump on the company jet had been improperly installed.

The president never said a word to me about the incident. But at the end of that month, I received a 50 percent "merit raise."

I Become a Psychic Spy

Things returned to normal, and I went back to predicting how customers would respond to new aerosol-can designs and other unromantic tasks. And I did finally get to work in a darkened room—not conducting a séance, but reviewing television commercials for foot powder, acne medicine, and denture cream adhesives. It was ghastly!

I must have sniffed a thousand different scents concocted by company chemists. At times it wasn't clear which they most valued—my sixth sense or my sense of smell!

It wouldn't be right to give the impression that a multimillion-dollar firm was relying solely on my intuition. Sometimes my employers took my advice, but many times my suggestions were overridden. In the vast majority of cases, however, when my recommendations were heeded, they paid off handsomely. And gradually my influence in the company grew.

You would hardly expect the work of a corporate seer to remain routine, though. It was a beautiful Monday morning in June when John West called me into his office—the inner sanctum, as his secretary jokingly referred to it.

He wasn't the sort of man to come directly to any point. For about twenty minutes he rambled on about everything from the price of gold to the movies he'd seen lately. So I casually occupied myself with pruning the thirsty plants that decorated the table next to my chair.

Finally he got down to business. "Shawn," he said seriously, "I want you to try something a little out of the ordinary."

"Not another mouthwash!" I moaned.

He smiled. "What about espionage—is that more to your taste?"

For a moment I was stunned. I couldn't picture John as a secret agent for the CIA or the KGB. Even when he wore his London Fog coat and smoked a pipe, he didn't look the part. But I should have realized that that wasn't the kind of espionage he had in mind.

"What I want you to do is to focus in on our competition. See if you can anticipate *their* sales figures. See if you can read their minds and tell us what new products they have under research and development."

"In other words," I replied, "you want me to be a psychic spy!"

"Yes, if you want to call it that. . . ."

I had my reservations. After all, it's against the law to tap a competitor's phone, tie into his computer lines, or buy secrets from his employees. But John convinced me that there was nothing illegal about psychic surveillance. It was just sneaky.

I admit that the promise of a bonus helped me make up my mind! And so I tuned in on all their competitors. I tried to project what their ad campaigns would emphasize, and what new scents and fragrances their scientists were working on. Once I even tried to "see" the secret ingredients in a competitor's herbal shampoo.

The results were difficult to evaluate. Telepathy is still not as reliable a form of communication as the telephone! And in predicting the future, there is always the problem of *when* a foreseen event is likely to happen. An extrasensory preception doesn't flash in the mind like a newsreel, a booming voice announcing "On August 4, 1973, a major competitor will introduce a line of shampoos that color the hair." The perceptions I receive are much more subtle and tentative—impressions, not detailed reports.

Sometimes I can sense *what*, but not *when*. Or *who*, but not *what*. Still, I was able to anticipate certain important trends in the industry—for instance, that there would be a reaction against aerosols because of their effect on the atmosphere. I also predicted the concern that would arise concerning the health hazards of artificial additives and colorings. And this was in 1972, long before it became commonplace for the FDA to withdraw suspect chemicals from the market.

A number of my predictions have yet to come true. I still anticipate that a midwestern company will introduce a toothpaste with a chemical that's far more effective than fluoride in preventing cavities. I believe that plastic containers will soon be replaced by a new lightweight, unbreakable material that requires less petroleum to manufacture. A French firm will discover the link between natural human fragrances and sexual attractiveness; the outcome of this research—but this is far in the future—will be a sensational line of perfumes with proven aphrodisiacal properties. I also look forward to the day when wrinkles and other outward signs of aging will be completely eliminated through the use of cosmetic hormones. This breakthrough should come before 1985.

The Great Hair-Spray Controversy

Psychic spying continued to be a regular part of my work load at XYZ—until the great hair-spray controversy indirectly brought my cosmetics career to a premature end.

At one of our regular product-evaluation meetings, I was given a sample of a new men's hair spray that they planned to distribute under their brand name. I immediately had a negative reaction to the product—almost an allergic blowup, you might say.

"You've considered other names for this product, haven't you?" I asked.

From the expressions on their faces I could tell I'd hit an exposed nerve. "How did she know that?" one of the marketing experts demanded to know. John looked uncomfortable.

"The other name that was under serious consideration had a manly, aggressive sound to it, didn't it?"

I regretted the question the minute I had asked it. "That is not your concern," snapped a testy young executive, reeking with the company's most expensive scent.

It didn't take a psychic to figure out that somebody's pride was at stake. So I gave my appraisal of the package as tersely as possible, concealing as best as I could the strong feeling I had that the product name was a serious mistake, and that the other name that I "knew" had been considered (and which they never revealed to me) was the name they should go with.

Later that afternoon I found out there had been a board-room battle between the pro- and anti-factions. Tempers had flared like Molotov cocktails. A number of high-living executives faced the prospect that their next check would be for $99.88 in unemployment compensation.

That night I dreamed that I too would be terminated, to use the grim corporate word for being fired.

Unhappily, my premonition came true only five days later. Before the pink slip arrived, I had already cleaned out my desk and prepared to leave.

There was a major purge, resembling those for which a famous executive was notorious. Several of my sponsors were among the victims. And despite the personal gratitude that the president may have felt toward me for the warning I had once given him—which had saved his life—he was unable, or unwilling, to protect me.

Part Two

On My Own

8

Declaring Myself

After I left, I was steadily unemployed, and agonized about what to do next. Part of me wanted to go out and find another nice, easy corporate job where I would feel safe and secure. And another part of me wanted to let my gift determine what path my life would follow.

All my friends urged me to become a professional psychic, insisting that in just a short while, people would learn about my power, and that soon I would be holding office hours just like a psychiatrist. But I was terrified to make such a move. What if no one came to me? How would I pay my rent and phone bills? It just didn't seem possible that I would be able to use this gift as a way to make a living.

As I moved slowly toward the decision to become a professional psychic, my contact with Maria became less and less frequent. Even though we were now living in the same city, she seldom contacted me anymore, and gradually her presence around me began to fade.

Of course, when I needed someone to talk to, she was always there—any time, day or night. When something troubled me, or when a terrible vision of death or disaster came, I knew I could call her and be soothed by the warmth of her love.

For months and months I couldn't make a decision. But within my heart, I could feel I was destined to become a professional. Even my own visions showed me that I would be working and earning my keep by helping people in their daily lives. There was only one career in which I could be happy.

I felt like an artist who loves to paint and knows that nothing else will ever make him happy, but who fears giving up his routine job. Like him, I knew I would be losing any security I had. You may be successful in fulfilling your life's dream, but meanwhile, you may also starve and go bankruput!

Returning Home

Time did not make matters any more clear, so I determined to take a vacation from the whole issue for a few weeks. I left my apartment and journeyed back to Queens to spend a few weeks alone with Mom and Dad.

I remember getting off the subway and walking through that lovely little neighborhood toward my parents' house. Many powerful memories flooded back into my mind.

I saw the spot where we found my friend's little dog dead that day so many years ago. I passed the park where four young men had pursued me that terrifying night. I remembered all the difficult and lonely years I had spent at my old high school, afraid to let any one know how different I was.

And when I reached the house, I was filled with emotions and saw visions of myself as a young child. This feeling was so powerful that it was as though I had died and was reliving my life.

Everything about the house had remained exactly the same. Only my parents looked older as they welcomed me inside.

My parents were amazingly understanding. Perhaps they were using their own psychic powers to see what was troubling me—for throughout those weeks I spent with them, they never once asked me why I had come home, what was troubling me, or why I hadn't looked for another job.

As I sat at the dinner table the first night home, my parents told me all about Helene's new husband and how happy she had been feeling lately. As we sat and ate my mother's brisket of beef, I could see in their loving eyes that they understood my current problem.

Although they were graying now, and their movements were slower, they seemed virtually unchanged by the years. Their level of understanding had not changed—we were still able to communicate without feeling the need to speak. I could sense that they knew what was bothering me and did not need to ask any questions.

The days passed uneventfully. I spent much of my time sitting alone in my room, surrounded by the dolls and teddy bears that had delighted me in childhood, simply trying to collect my thoughts and feelings. With each day I grew more certain that my only choice was that of the psychic life. I tried to picture myself going on to another corporate job, but that, my visions showed me, would never happen.

And so I was almost ready to make my decision. I was on the brink of declaring myself a professional psychic to the world. And whether I would fail or succeed, I was willing to give it a try.

"Don't Be Afraid"

But I still had lingering doubts. And I decided to confront this hesitance.

That day, my mother sat in the living room working on her needlepoint as an album of classical music played quietly on the stereo, and rays of sunlight streamed in through the window. She did not turn to watch me coming down the stairs, but she could sense I was there.

I went into the kitchen and poured two cups of coffee from the pot on the stove. Her coffee tasted rich and delicious, as always.

I went and sat beside her on the sofa in the living room. Sensing, even before I spoke, that I needed to talk, she put her needlepoint aside. "You've got a big decision to make," she said, already knowing what was troubling me.

"It's so hard, Mom. I know what I should do. My visions tell me what to do. And yet I'm still afraid. . . ."

"Don't be afraid, Shawn. You know, when you were little I knew you had a very special talent. I knew you would never be just an average person; I feared the troubles and loneliness ahead, so I tried to discourage you from developing your gift. But it didn't work. Your powers were always too strong to be ignored. And I knew sooner or later this day would come."

I felt like a little girl crying to her mother, "Tell me what to do."

"You *already* know what you have to do. You have to trust yourself, Shawn. You have to put away these fears that reflect the attitudes of society. Your visions tell you to become a professional psychic, don't they?"

"Yes," I answered, amazed at how well she knew my thoughts.

"Then there's nothing to consider. Go ahead. Your visions have been good to you so far, haven't they?"

I stopped for a moment and thought about my life. Mother was right: My visions never *had* failed me on an important decision. More than once in fact, my visions had probably saved my life!

"Go ahead," she said kindly. The sun, moving through the sky, threw the golden beam of light closer to where we sat. "Go ahead and be bold. I'm sure it will all work out. If in time you feel you made the wrong decision, you can always go back. You're young and you can experiment with these alternatives. Later in life you may not be able to."

Now my path was clear. From that moment on, I felt there was no alternative and no turning back.

I left the house the next day, feeling a little sad as I kissed my parents good-bye at the front door. But I was also happy about having spent those days with them, and very excited about this new life opening up for me.

Returning to Manhattan, I immediately went to share the good news with my friend Jane, who believed deeply in my powers. I had done several readings for her and many of her close friends. Now she assured me that she and those friends would be my first clients.

A New Apartment for a New Life

Although I loved the little space I had been living in, I now needed a bigger place where I could live and also do business. So Jane and I began searching the city for a new apartment.

After several days of combing the newspapers, pounding the pavement, knocking on doors, and calling real-estate agents, we found the perfect spot—an apartment of good size, without being too large or impersonal. The cozy and relaxing living room was not big, but it had a working fireplace and lots of windows—a perfect place, I thought, for personal readings.

The bedroom gave me lots of space for privacy. And the kitchen was painted bright yellow and was full of sunlight. Leasing an apartment, though, is a big decision you don't run into blindly.

The landlady, who had come with us to show off the apartment, was in her sixties, with hair white as snow and a crooked back that made her lean forward. She spoke slowly, with a heavy German accent, but her voice expressed a great charm and a deeply loving nature.

As she talked to us, I got wonderful feelings about her, I saw that she and I would become good friends in the future. But still wanting to be professional about our business relationship, I asked a great many questions about the apartment. How often would it be painted? Did the heat work well?

She answered all my questions courteously, and then showed me a copy of the lease. Jane and I combined our brains and decided that it looked just fine.

For a final moment I paused, looking at the charming little apartment, tottering at the brink of saying yes and signing the dotted line.

At that moment, all at once the sun came out from behind the clouds, and a lovely beam of light came streaming through the windows. Instantly my mind flashed back to the conversation I'd had with my mother, and I heard her voice telling me that everything would be all right. And I turned to charming old Mrs. Jenkins and said yes.

About to sign the lease, Mrs. Jenkins began asking *me* a few questions. I told her about growing up in Queens, about my last apartment. Finally she asked me what I did for a living.

For the first time in my life, I told a *stranger* that I was a professional psychic—and right away I could tell she was shocked, wondering if I'd be hanging signs out the window saying Palms Read, like a carnival gypsy. Mrs. Jenkins was a devout *non*believer in psychic phenomena, and most certainly did not believe that I had any special powers.

It took a little doing to convince her that I would not be bringing sailors into her apartment house for fast crystal-ball consultations, nor would I disturb the other tenants in any way. After all, my daily work is not unlike that of a doctor. Respectable people come to see me at prearranged hours. Psychics are quite considerate of other tenants, and clean!

Finally convinced that she had nothing to fear, Mrs. Jenkins let me sign the lease. But she still considered me a little crazy, and certainly did not believe in my gift.

I Move In—and Meet Kisser

The next few weeks were absolute chaos, as I moved all my furniture to the new apartment. Painting, cleaning, getting things in shape, I was also calling all my old friends to tell them about my career change, and hoping that they would soon become clients.

One damp, dreary day during those weeks of settling in, I was walking around the neighborhood—supposedly looking for furniture. But really I was just wandering, lost in thought, wondering how soon it would rain.

It was getting dark. The sun had gone down just a few moments before, and the city took on that beautiful texture that comes when the lights are first turned on and the sky is turning a deep red. The air was misty and cool, and I realized it was time to head for home.

I was passing an alley between two buildings, and not knowing why, I turned to look in. It was dark and threatening, filled with garbage cans and dangerous shadows. Among the debris lay a small cat, crying and obviously in need of help.

Walking cautiously into the dark alley, I could see that there was blood on her fur. She looked hungry, frightened, and alone.

I lifted her gently into my arms. On her side, I could feel more blood, and dampness from the wet sidewalk. She didn't resist my touch, but instead seemed to sense that I wanted to help her. It sounds strange, but at that moment it was almost as though I could hear her thanking me. I took the injured little animal back to my apartment and found the wound under her fur where she was bleeding. After cleaning it gently with a little soap and water, I covered it with a piece of clean cotton.

I knew she must be starving, so I tried to scrounge something up from the kitchen that might appeal to her.

I remembered my childhood pet cat who only lived with us a few years, late in her life, before passing on. She'd always loved to eat eggs beaten into some fresh milk. Since this was about all I had in my constantly barren refrigerator, I thought I'd give it a try. But she was so hungry she would probably have eaten a dog biscuit! After devouring the egg in one gulp, she crawled slowly back into the living room and fell asleep on the couch. The next day I took her to a veterinarian to have her tended to.

I named her Kisser because she insists on nuzzling everyone who comes into my apartment. Since then, Kisser has been my constant roommate and one of my closest friends.

One of her stranger habits is a burning desire to be photographed. Whenever someone comes to take pictures—whether it be a newspaper reporter, a TV journalist, or filmmaker—Kisser leaps up into my lap just as the shutter is about to open. With this careful timing, she has managed to get her face onto the pages of many major newspapers and magazines.

Amazingly, the first few weeks provided Kisser with an opportunity to return my kindness in full. One evening I had been up late working on the apartment, as usual. I was in the middle of painting the kitchen, and while waiting for the first coat to dry, decided to make some coffee.

I turned on the gas on the stove, then went out to the living room to wait for the pot to perk. But when I eased down into my favorite armchair, I soon had trouble keeping my eyes open. Hoping reading might help me stay awake, I began scouring the day's newspaper, as I always do, for articles about the world situation.

But it was no use. Within a few moments I fell off to sleep, letting the second coat of paint go for another day.

But a tugging at my feet soon roused me. Unwillingly I opened one eye and looked down. Kisser was biting my shoe. Being in no mood for games, I tried to chase her away, and began to drift off again. But she persisted, tugging and swatting at me with determination.

Quite aggravated, I got up to chase her away. Then I noticed the smell—the entire apartment was filled with the odor of gas!

I got up and ran to kitchen. The pilot light was out, and the burner under my coffeepot had never ignited. Gasping for air, I shut off the burner, ran to the window, and threw it open.

As soon as I felt stronger, I opened all the other windows in the apartment. Just now returning from the haziness of sleep, I began to wonder what had stirred me in the first place.

Then I looked down to see Kisser mewing at my feet. The sad litle cat, whom I had saved from a lonely death just a few weeks before, had now returned the favor. Kisser and I have been dearest pals ever since.

I had just begun a new career that offered no security and doubtful success, and already I had a second mouth to feed. Fortunately, it wasn't long before things began to pick up for Kisser and me.

Making a Start

Soon I had a fairly busy schedule. Old friends whom I had read for before were now coming to the apartment, and began recommending me to others as well. I was seeing two or three people every day for personal consultations.

At first it was hard to bring myself to charge these people

money for my services. After all, for years I had done readings like this absolutely free, and I had no way of knowing what a psychic was expected to charge. Should I consider myself to be on a par with a psychiatrist and ask for fifty, even sixty dollars an hour? Or should I just expect to get the same hourly rate that I had earned as a secretary?

Since I couldn't make a decision, I finally began telling people to give me whatever they thought I was worth. And the amounts absolutely amazed me. For a one-hour reading, some people paid me as much as one hundred dollars.

But on the average I received a great deal less than that. And after a while, when I knew how much most people were prepared to spend, I was able to decide on a fixed rate for my work.

I wasn't getting rich, but I was happier than I had ever been before in my life. It was as if a weight had been lifted from my back. All those years of playing with the band and then working for a corporation, I had always felt that something was wrong, that I was supposed to be somewhere else, doing something more important.

Now that I had finally declared myself to the world, I felt free. And although I still felt a great need to be cautious and responsible about the advice I gave, I knew I was doing the right thing, helping people, leading them in the right directions.

And with the exercise, I could feel my powers growing stronger and sharper. Just as a typist will become faster and more accurate with work, so as I gained more experience, I became able to have clearer, more exact visions for my clients.

For most clients I soon found that I could call up a vision on command. When in the past I had simply conversed with people and waited for something to come to me, I began to let people ask questions. Now clients could ask me about something very specific—a career or love—and I could focus my mind on that exact aspect of their life and find an image to answer their question.

I did well, to say the least. In those first few months of my career, I began to get phone calls from other professional psychics, welcoming me to the group, so to speak. They were kind and encouraging, and often invited me to meetings that took place from time to time.

Mrs. Jenkins Changes Her Mind

My relationship with my landlady remained pleasant but strained. I would often see her in the lobby of the building, and we would talk for a moment or two.

I could see the doubt in her eyes. She didn't have to utter a single word in her heavy accent to tell me that she thought I was a fake.

I would pass her, say hello, head toward the elevator, and I could practically hear her talking to herself (in German, of course) about these strange American customs. But she was the kind of person who believed in being courteous and polite at all times, even when talking to outrageous charlatans like myself; and despite her feelings, she remained sweet and charming.

A few weeks after I moved in, I had a problem with the hot water, and I went down to Mrs. Jenkins' apartment to tell her about it. When she arrived at the door I had a sudden sense that something was wrong. As had happened to me before with friends and clients, I received a very distinct psychic image from her that could mean only one thing—illness.

While telling her about the hot-water problem, I tried to get a more specific idea of what might be wrong with her. Within a few moments I got a very distinct vision of a small, malignant cancer developing in her right arm, near the surface. And probably she had skin cancer as well. I paused, knowing there was no way in the world that she would believe me. But it was my obligation to tell her, whether she believed me or not.

"Mrs. Jenkins, I know you won't believe me, but I'm getting a psychic feeling about you. I sense that there is a small cancer developing on your right arm. It is malignant but tiny, and if you take action now and go to a doctor, he will be able to remove it easily without any possibility of a recurrence. I know you think I'm a fake, and that you don't believe in psychic phenomena, but I wish you'd at least take the time to just go to see a doctor—if only to prove to yourself that I'm wrong and my powers are false."

I wasn't sure what her reaction would be to all this, but I

was hoping that my concern would motivate her to visit a doctor.

As it turned out, her son was a physician who came to visit her every week or two. The next time he dropped by, she told him my "ridiculous" story.

That afternoon, when I opened the door, I saw a pleasant-looking young man with curly, dark hair and a pleasant smile. "Ms. Robbins, my name is Dr. Jenkins, Mrs. Jenkins' son. May I come in?"

I immediately invited him in, and offered him a glass of wine. He asked me a few questions about my work, and I told him all I could, being completely honest.

"My mother told me what you said to her. She thought the whole thing very silly. I took a look at her arm, and I can't say for certain yet, but it does look like a very small cancer is beginning to develop and spread. I think you were correct. I'm taking her over to the hospital this afternoon for an examination."

Even though Mrs. Jenkins had a fairly low opinion of me, I liked her very much and wanted her to be healthy.

"Do you have some knowledge of medicine, Ms. Robbins? Have you been medically trained?"

"No, I haven't, doctor. And I would never attempt to prescribe any form of treatment or medication. I don't pretend to be able to do *your* job. If I sense illness in my clients or friends, I simply recommend that they see a doctor as soon as possible."

"Please don't misunderstand me. I'm not trying to cross-examine you. In fact, I want to thank you for pointing out my mother's illness. And I am simply amazed at the accuracy of your prediction. You must be a very gifted person."

Mrs. Jenkins' cancer was easily removed and did not return. Had she waited much longer, however, the situation could have become far more serious.

A few weeks later, when she returned from the hospital to her apartment, she called me immediately and invited me to come down.

This was the first time I'd seen her apartment, and I was absolutely charmed. The walls were literally covered with pictures of Dr. Jenkins, from his naked childhood bottom on a bearskin rug to his graduation from Harvard Medical School.

The furnishings were quite old, but absolutely exquisite. I'm sure every piece in the room was an antique, probably worth a fortune.

Mrs. Jenkins was so overwhelmed with gratitude that she was on the verge of tears. I told her over and over that she was welcome, and tried to assure her that when I warned her, I was only doing what I had to, more for my own conscience than anything else.

But she insisted that I had saved her life, that I was a saint, God's messenger on earth, and so on.

As it turned out, that single piece of advice probably did as much good for me as it did for her. From that day forward, she began sending all her friends to me for advice.

And Dr. Jenkins also started recommending me to his colleagues at the hospital, as well as to other professional people—lawyers, politicians, businessmen.

So in that one moment of revelation, I not only made a new believer, I had begun a career.

9
Recognition by the Enquirer

By the early 1970s, I was committed to the professional life. As time went on, I was reading for more and more people. And I discovered that by using my gift in this way, I could make enough money to live on.

Things were moving slowly, but I was happy to finally be doing what I had always sensed I must. I took pleasure in my work, even when it brought sadness, glad to be helping as many people as I could.

But I was still virtually unknown, reading only for friends and acquaintances. On rare occasions a stranger who had heard of my abilities would come to me. And yet my first major recognition did not come because I wanted it. Instead, sooner than I expected, I was forced into the limelight of national exposure when the *National Enquirer* reported my premonition of an airline disaster, as I've related in Chapter 1. But in my profession, recognition is a double-edged sword. On the one hand, everyone wants to be appreciated. And the more recognition a psychic attracts, the more seriously his or her predictions will be taken. But if I was in this life primarily to help people, why should I be so concerned about fame and money? That question continues to trouble my conscience.

With the coming of recognition, my life began to change drastically. I found myself receiving so many more requests for personal consultation that I was forced to turn some down. Articles and columns about my work continued to appear in the *Enquirer,* and other newspapers started contacting me as well.

Only a few months after my prediction of the DC-10 crash, I received my first invitation to appear on a radio talk show to be broadcast on a local New York channel. At first I hesitated, but my friends and family unanimously insisted that I accept the invitation.

The host of the show was really quite charming; it was his business to get people to relax and to get them to talk. But despite his expert kindness, I was terrified. I have always had a tendency to suffer stage fright, even in the years when I was performing as a musician. And now being out there alone, the center of attention, I was so nervous that I could barely speak.

This was a call-in talk show, and soon the phones were opened to accept listeners' questions. I was truly amazed to discover how many people are interested in receiving psychic advice. And I was also shocked to discover how many of the callers already knew about me because of the prediction I had made concerning the crash of the DC-10.

As the callers spoke, I had no trouble getting visions concerning most of them. I had never really tried reading for someone I hadn't yet met, so I was delighted to find that the process of prediction worked even over the telephone.

As I spoke, I tried my best to make the callers open up and relax, just as I do during a personal reading in my own home. I have always found that a little humor or kidding calms people down, and if you can find a way to make people laugh at their own problems, you have half the battle won. It's this kind of relaxation on both sides that tends to lead to accurate predictions.

Well, this first radio appearance was a success, and I would be invited back several times. Other stations began calling me too, and making this kind of personal appearance became a major part of my life.

By this time my career was busy with as many readings as I could handle. My predictions were being published in the *Enquirer,* and I was doing a few radio shows a week. I didn't think there was much more that could happen to me.

On the Air!

But there was, and it was called television.

If I had been nervous during a radio appearance, I was downright terrified on talk panels, wondering what to do with my hands, gulping before each sentence, wondering if anyone would notice how much I was perspiring.

But thank God, my first TV spot was a success. And the next day, all the friends who had watched it said, hard as it may be to believe, they were most impressed with how cool and calm I had remained, as though I had been making television appearances all my life. If they had only known that in reality I had been trying to figure out how to keep myself from throwing up during prime time!

As my professional life continued to grow and expand, I never really experienced any major setbacks. Once people are convinced of your power, they will seek your help. And the amount of publicity a psychic receives at any given time doesn't seem to have any big effect.

Climbing the Fence to Success

I was now doing more and more TV and radio broadcasts in New York, and even beginning to do shows in other cities.

It seems that not long before a television show I did in Boston, there had been a robbery in the city. Although the police had captured the criminals, they had not yet found the stolen cash.

They had assumed that the money was somewhere between the point where the criminals had been arrested and the site of the robbery, but they had been searching for several days without finding anything.

The host of the TV show asked me if I thought I could help the police locate the money. "Of course I can't be certain I'll be able to," I told him, "but there's a good chance I could. I'll be happy to try."

The next day the local police took me to where the robbery had occurred. Along with a team of bloodhounds, we retraced the path to the spot where the arrest had taken place. I tried to pick up some feelings about where the criminals had been and where they might have dropped their loot. But surrounded by the din of barking dogs and all those doubtful policemen, it was a little difficult to concentrate.

The path we were following led away from the houses and shops near the robbery scene and off into the surrounding woods. The criminals had obviously believed they would be safer away from streets and people.

I could feel the path the criminals had taken, but the dogs found the trail a lot faster than I did and remained hot on the trail.

Soon we were approaching a fence running just about as far as the eye could see. One officer told me that the fence had apparently deterred the robbers. Rather than jump over it, they had followed alongside it for some distance. Somehow, I sensed that this assumption was not correct. I told the officer I could see the two crooks jumping over the fence in a panic. He paid little attention to my remark.

But just then, the dogs proved me right. They ran to the fence, sniffing all the way, and stopped. The policeman beside me now was a little embarrassed. I told him not to be—who really believes in psychics anyway?

Well, a new problem now arose. How we were all to get over the fence that lay before us?

I'm in quite good shape physically, so it was not the physical climb that posed a problem. My difficulty was emotional. I haven't mentioned it before, but perhaps my greatest phobia is that of heights. I was too frightened to climb.

Well, the officers had been a little disgruntled about this whole affair before, and you can imagine how they felt now. Here, afraid to climb a fence, was the psychic who was going to find the hidden money! As it turned out, the officers had to actually lift me over. Even this frightened me!

Only a short distance from the other side of the fence, though, I sensed something nearby, and soon found the money stashed under a tree. This moment of triumph at least offset my earlier embarrassment—and it came none too soon!

Since then, before taking off in hot pursuit of criminals, I always make sure there are no fences involved.

At Last, Mr. Right

Then, a few years ago, I finally met the man of my dreams.

Ironically, I knew Frank Darling (not his real name) long before we actually met. During the last year or so of my musical career, I seemed to hear his name wherever I went.

When the band arrived in a new town, we usually got settled at the hotel first, and then headed over to whatever club we were playing to meet the manager and investigate the clientele and the acoustics.

When you first arrive, nightclub managers tend to try their best to put you on the defensive. They like to tell you about how well the last act did that played the club, and what you must measure up to.

Hundreds of times, it seems, our band came into a town right on the heels of Frank, an actor who often toured with various plays and revues. Countless times we would listen to a club manager say, "We had Frank Darling in here last week. He was sensational." Normally I would not have appreciated this kind of information, but somehow I was fascinated by this actor I'd never met. Neither Frank nor I were working as psychics at that time. But somehow I knew that our paths would cross, that we would meet one day, and that he would be the perfect man for me. And I was correct on all counts.

Several years later, after I had made the career change from music to personal advisor, a friend came to my apartment for dinner.

We sat in the living room, drinking Burgundy and listening to jazz records, when she mentioned another psychic she had met recently. The moment she mentioned his name was Frank Darling I was overwhelmed with very positive psychic feelings about this man whom I had not yet met. The vision was so powerful, so positive, that I decided that instant to try to meet Mr. Darling as soon as possible. I asked my friend to get his phone number and called him up the very next day.

Once on the phone with Frank, my feelings about him grew more intense still. It was a lot like love at first sight, except that I hadn't even seen him yet!

He lived only a few blocks away from my apartment, so I asked him to have dinner with me at a Japanese restaurant in the area—a convenient meeting place for both of us.

A Proposal of Marriage

That evening in the restaurant, we talked and talked for hours. You might be amazed to discover how freely and openly two psychics can converse. Much of the communication isn't even spoken. When two people with ESP (and other psychic powers) get together, they can become old friends within a few short minutes.

We talked about Frank's background. An Englishman by birth, he spent most of his early years studying to be an actor. He was actually something of a child genius, receiving acclaim and awards. Later he went on to study acting in Canada. By the time he was an adolescent, he was already producing and acting in plays, radio dramas, and television shows. In addition, he was an expert in speech therapy, and had worked for several Canadian government agencies. Later, while working with stroke victims in California hospitals, his discovery that he was often able to communicate with these people nonverbally led him to become fascinated with the study of parapsychology. He arranged to meet with some of the world's top psychics and astrologers, who were convinced that Frank did indeed have psychic powers. Within a short time, he became a professional psychic like myself, and was soon a well-known public figure both here and in Europe.

We had so much in common that it was truly astounding. I found, for instance, that we are both interested in the teachings of Zen Buddhism—and he fits to a tee my image of a truly handsome man. In fact, he is even more handsome than I envisioned my perfect man to be!

Through dinner we talked and talked, and it was quite clear to both of us that we would be more than just friends. I could see Frank's thoughts as he wondered whether to turn the conversation to more personal matters.

But I took the first bold step on my own: "We have so much in common, Frank. Why don't we get married?"

Incredible as it may seem, after years and years of virtual celibacy, I proposed to this man on our first date.

And perhaps even more incredibly, he accepted! I think it was a case of two people simply *knowing* without a doubt that they belonged together. I am sure his feelings about me were just as positive as my impressions of him.

And so we became engaged. My friends and family were all a little surprised that I was rushing into marriage, and I understood their concern—not many get engaged on the first date!

Opposite Sides of the World

But as it turned out, our visions of a life together were only partially accurate. For in the months of our engagement we found ourselves dragged to opposite sides of the world, and we seldom had the opportunity to be together. Frank was always heading back to England to appear on a TV show, or to do some personal readings. And I was often going to California or some other part of the United States, either for personal work or to aid some distant police department. This constant separation led us to decide that marriage would not be the right arrangement for us. In this aspect, our original impressions concerning our life together were wrong, and yet we do share our lives with one another. Frank is still my closest friend, and I love him very much. I could say that I think he feels the same way about me, but that would not be true—I *know* he feels the same as I do! Every chance we get, Frank and I are together to share our troubles, victories, and questions about the future. We often work together, or sit together in my apartment composing folk songs or telling stories. Although I know now that I will never marry, I also know that I have indeed found that perfect man, and that he is my friend and colleague as well.

We often get chances to do some delightful projects together. Recently, for instance, a reporter from a New York magazine, a racehorse handicapper, Frank, and I went out to the racetracks in a psychic experiment to see who could pick the winning horses. The reporter was relying on luck, the handicapper on his expertise, and Frank and I used our psychic powers. Well, he and I spent so much of our time talking that we came in last! Since this was one of the few chances we had to be together, we were simply enjoying each other's company so much that we never really concentrated on the business at hand.

I am not unhappy about the way my romantic life has worked out. A more satisfying one is possible, but I am certain that mine is the right one for me. As demanding and unusual as my work is, I doubt that even Frank could really live with me. Romance seems to be just another of those things that I have been forced to forego in order to pursue my gift. But each time I help someone solve a problem, or steer someone in the right direction, I think of all the love and affection I have sacrificed. And for a moment I feel a little sad—but only for a moment.

10
My Most Important Predictions

During the last decade I've made thousands of predictions. Some proved false, but most have been frighteningly accurate. Often I am asked to list which of my predictions I consider my most important. But what makes a prediction "important"? Is accuracy the deciding factor? Can importance be measured by the size of the tragedy, or the number of people killed? Or are my most important predictions those which were heeded in time, helping someone avoid trouble, or even disaster?

In the end, when categorizing my predictions, I am completely subjective. The most important are ones I shall never forget: predictions concerning crashes, bombings, world events, and police cases. Some led to positive actions, such as the capture of criminals. But unfortunately, most of my major predictions have been ignored, and the tragedies came to pass just as I had foreseen.

Most of the ten predictions I consider my most outstanding are visions of terrible death and disaster that will haunt me for the rest of my life. Some precognitions helped establish to the world the validity of my work. But all concern tragic events, and I would gladly have sacrificed the fame these visions brought me if the tragedy could have been avoided. I wish each one of these predictions had been false!

Number One: A DC-10 Will Crash

For reasons unknown to me, I seem to be uniquely attuned to air disasters, so it is not inappropriate, I suppose, that my first important prediction described what was at the time the worst air tragedy in aviation history. In 1974 I was working in New York with the psychic Bob Brown (not his real name) undergoing hypnosis and testing my powers. During a trance I described to Bob a terrible plane crash in which hundreds would be killed and no one would survive. I told him that the plane, en route to London, would be destroyed by a terrorist bomb smuggled on board, and would crash into a forest. I also gave a rough date for the crash: either March or May of that year. And I saw that an American diplomat and his wife would be on board, and—along with all the other passengers—would not survive.

Overwhelmed by the energy and fear I showed, Bob advised me to contact the FBI immediately and tell them about my dream. The next day, we went together to the FBI's New York offices and talked with an officer of the aviation division. As I described my prediction to the officer, another detail came to me: I saw a large *T* on a piece of the wreckage that covered the quiet forest scene, surrounded by hundreds of dead, mutilated passengers.

To my surprise, the officer was genuinely interested in my vision. I had always assumed that policemen and government officials would have little interest in the forewarnings psychics communicate. But this FBI man seemed to believe my words. He showed me dozens of pictures of known terrorists, in the hope I might be able to recognize one of them as the bomber. Unfortunately, none of the faces made a strong impression on me.

After giving him all the details I could recall, we left. The officer promised to investigate the case fully, and I told him that if any more details came to me I would contact him right away, and offered to stay available for any further questions he might have.

And so I waited—nervously, hoping my prediction would not come true. All day long I listened anxiously to the news, dreading the report of a disaster I sensed was inevitable.

Twelve days after my meeting with the FBI, a Turkish Airlines DC-10 traveling from Paris to London crashed in the French countryside. A terrorist bomb *had* caused the crash. No one survived, and among the 346 people killed were an American diplomat and his wife.

My vision had been astonishingly accurate, even down to the *T* (in the lettering TURKISH AIRLINES on the side of the destroyed plane's body).

From that time on, my life was filled with these occasional predictions of terrifying tragedy. And while I have come to accept my peculiar role as prophet of doom, I have never learned to overcome the terrible fear and depression that these visions bring on.

Number Two: Terrorism Again

Later in 1974 I had another vision of terrorist activity that seemed so real, so immediate, that I knew it must be a premonition. I was home in my apartment, taking a shower, when suddenly I heard a man's voice with a thick Irish accent. He was talking to a Brittish official, identified himself as a member of the IRA, and said that he would soon bomb the Houses of Parliament in London: The bomb would be set and exploded before August of that year.

My vision was reported in the *National Enquirer*, and again I made attempts to contact various officials who might be able to prevent this terrorist act. Unfortunately, they were unable to, and on June 17, 1974, a bomb blast ripped through the honored walls of the Houses of Parliament. Luckily, it was still early morning, and few of the lords had appeared; the other government employees had not yet reported to work. Only eleven persons were injured, and no one was killed. Within hours of the blast, government officials received a phone call from IRA members claiming responsibility.

Again my reputation grew, as reports of my prediction

were published in newspapers and magazines. And again, I would have gladly forfeited this fame to have been able to prevent it.

Number Three: Patty Hearst

A year later, in 1975, the kidnapped daughter of the publishing magnate, who had apparently become an urban terrorist, was the subject of the largest (and perhaps least successful) manhunt in American history.

I was appearing on a television show in Washington, D.C., on WTOP-TV. The interviewer asked me a great many questions about famous movie and television stars, and we fielded questions from the audience. Suddenly Patty Hearst came to my mind. I could "see" her being apprehended by the police. I sensed that she was near her home, perhaps in San Francisco. I also got an image of the date of her capture: It seemed to be mid-September of 1975, perhaps the eighteenth or nineteenth of the month.

When he heard my prediction, the TV show host was far from shocked. Psychics all over the world had been making numerous—largely incorrect—predictions of her capture for some months. The papers had been filled with stories and rumors about her whereabouts and her activities, and so my prediction sounded like one among hundreds.

But Patty Hearst was apprehended in San Francisco on September 18, 1975. In my prediction I had also mentioned that I thought she would go to jail for a short while and then be placed on probation for three years. As she was.

This was the kind of major prediction I was happy to make: no one was harmed, justice was served, and my reputation strengthened—a good prediction in every way.

Number Four: Another Plane Crash

In May of 1975 one of my airline dreams roused me from my sleep and frightened me terribly. Since by this time I was submitting predictions to the *National Enquirer* on a regular basis, I wrote down this latest prediction and sent it to them. The crash, I told them, would be one of the worst in American history, with over one hundred people killed in a single plane. The airline would be Eastern, the crash would occur in July or June of 1975, and it would take place at New York's Kennedy International Airport.

When the paper received my note, they naturally asked me for any additional details I could provide. I told them simply what I had sensed: In my dream I was aboard an airplane, when suddenly the entire craft began to shake violently. The shaking continued for what felt like an eternity; finally it stopped. Then I saw that the plane had crashed, leaving hundreds of bodies strewn over the airstrip. I saw the word *Eastern* printed on a part of the plane, and when I looked around I recognized the location to be Kennedy Airport. I could give no more details, except that there might be a thunderstorm during the crash.

The *Enquirer* ran the story, and one evening I met with an Eastern official and his wife and told them of my vision. Since my past record had already established accuracy, the Eastern official seemed to believe me and assured me he would do all he could. But the disaster still took place, ending just the way I had foreseen. On June 24, 1975, Eastern Airlines Flight 66 crashed at Kennedy Airport. More than one hundred of the passengers on board were killed instantly—the result of a violent summer thunderstorm that was raging over New York City that fateful June day. And again I wished that my accurate vision had been wrong.

A Few Weeks Later, Number Five

This time, too, the vision concerned an airport, but not a plane crash. Instead, I had a troubling feeling that at La Guardia Airport a terrorist bombing would take the lives of eleven innocent travelers.

In August of 1975 I was on a university's radio show in New York when the image of this wasteful and meaningless act of political murder first came to me. I instantly recognized La Guardia Airport, and knew that many passersby would be killed or injured when the bomb went off. I thought it would be set to go off around Christmastime of that year.

This vision upset me so that I was unable to complete my part of the interview. Again I informed New York City officials of the tragedy I foresaw, and prayed that it would never come to pass. But on December 29, 1975, a bomb went off in La Guardia Airport, killing eleven people and injuring several more.

Within days I was contacted by the FBI, who were desperately trying to find some clue that might lead them to the terrorists who had set the bomb. Sadly, I could give them no information about the criminals involved. For reasons still not completely clear to me, the FBI confiscated the original tape recording of that radio program. I do not think they were attempting to suppress information, but were trying to avoid any information leak that might harm their investigation or even prevent them from apprehending the killers.

Soon the headlines appeared: "Shawn Robbins Predicts Airport Bombing," "Shawn Robbins Has Amazingly Accurate Precognition." My fame was spreading rapidly. But at the expense of eleven innocent lives, it was not the kind of fame that could bring me joy.

Number Six: Among the Missing

My next important prediction did not concern an earth-shattering disaster, yet it made me feel I had been able to truly help someone I loved. One day an old high-school friend came to see me in my New York apartment. I was surprised to see her, especially since she had never placed any faith in my powers when we had both been younger. She looked lovely, truly striking with her jewelry and expensive clothes. Apparently she had a certain amount of material success in her life—she told me of her marriage to a wealthy lawyer in New Jersey, where they now lived with their three children. For a moment I even envied her simple, secure lifestyle, until I realized that a life like that would be impossible for me.

Soon, however, I learned that she had lost something far more valuable than any material objects. It seems that her father—a man I had known well as a child—had been missing for several weeks. She and her family were worried sick about him. The police had been trying to locate him, but with no luck. She said that she and her family would prefer knowing that her father was dead to living with the agony of wondering and waiting.

As she spoke, a powerful vision came to me. I could see her father's murdered body lying in the back seat of a large, green car somewhere in midtown New York.

My friend went to the police with this information, and they began an intensive search for the green car I had described. But after several days of investigation the car had still not turned up.

My friend called me and asked if I might be mistaken. "It's certainly possible for me to make a mistake," I told her, but even as I was speaking with her, the image of her father lying dead in that car returned—even stronger than before. "I still have the same vision," I told her, and urged her not to give up the search.

In my heart, however, I too began to doubt the accuracy of my prediction. Perhaps I had the car's color wrong? Or the section of the city was wrong? I could not be sure. Yet the vision I had first "seen" kept returning to me for days.

A few weeks later, while investigating an illegally parked truck in a private midtown garage, the police happened to look into the back. There they discovered the green car I had described. In the back seat of the car lay my friend's father, now dead several weeks. The autopsy showed that he had, in fact, been murdered. When I learned this, I tried my best to find some psychic clue to the murderer's identity or motive. Unfortunately, I was unable to give any more information.

I soon received a note from my friend. It was very hard for her family to accept their loss, but they were grateful that the previous weeks of desperate waiting were now over.

It is true that I had not been able to save my friend's father—I could not even help bring his murderer to justice. And yet I had helped her reach the truth and had brought an end to what had seemed like an endless wait. To me, helping someone I love through a terrible time in her life is one of the most important achievements of my career.

Often I stop to reflect how lucky I am that my powers are not even stronger, or every day of my life might be plagued with dreams and visions of disaster—a burden I truly could not cope with. As it is, every few months these terrible visions come to me, and at times I feel I'll never get beyond the depressions they bring on—that perhaps I will lose my perspective on reality or have a nervous breakdown. At such times, the help of my friends and family is most important to me. With their support, I manage to go on.

Number Seven: Murder!

The next major prediction I made came in 1977, and again concerned murder in cold blood.

A man named Alvin Richard (not his real name) had disappeared. The New York City Police had investigated, but could find no clues concerning his whereabouts. Don Gordon (not his real name), then of the New York police department's famed "Batman and Robin" team, came to my apartment and showed me a picture of the missing man. At the time, Don did not identify himself as a policeman—I assumed that he was simply one of the missing man's relatives. The moment I saw Mr. Richard's picture, I knew he had been murdered. Assuming this news would come as a shock to his "relative," I asked him to sit down before I gave him the bad news. As I began to speak, details concerning the crime came racing into my consciousness. I told Don that the body had been hidden in a garbage dump on Staten Island, and I described exactly where Mr. Richard's remains could be found.

I then went on to describe an apartment house in Brooklyn where I believed the murderer was living—for a change, I was even able to give details about what he looked like. I sensed that he had killed twice before, and that both of his other victims had been

Oriental. Even though he didn't seem upset by my feeling that Mr. Richard had been murdered, I think Don was shocked by my words. Soon he identified himself as a police detective, and within hours he was following up on what details I had been able to give him.

First, the police searched the garbage dump I had described, but were unable to find the body. This discouraged me—and Don as well. But he still had faith in my abilities, and decided to investigate the apartment house I had described.

Within two weeks, after an intensive stakeout, he arrested a man who soon confessed to Mr. Richard's murder. He admitted to having dumped the body in a garbage-disposal truck that regularly takes its contents to the Staten Island dump—just as I had foreseen. But what had happened to the body once it was taken there, no one knew—and it has not been found to this day. The murderer also admitted that he had killed two young Japanese women in Manhattan. He was convicted of murder and sentenced to life in prison.

It would be hard to say that this prediction made me happy. I had been unable to prevent three people from being murdered, and yet, helping bring the murderer to justice gave me some degree of satisfaction. Don Gordon went on to become a private investigator, and later a New York State assemblyman. The murderer is now serving time in a New York State penitentiary.

What makes a prediction an important one? The seven I have described so far are those which gained the most publicity, or brought widespread recognition of my powers. But for the most part, they brought sadness as well. But I know these tales tend to fascinate people. They look at these visions of doom as conclusive proof that psychic powers are valid.

And yet, I wonder if in the end, the everyday predictions I make in personal consultation are not more important. For these predictions, as unimpressive as they may seem, have a positive effect. When I give clients advice, they take my recommendations to heart. And in this way, I seem to be able to do good in this world.

Number Eight: Another Dream of Doom

Within a few months of my work with detective Gordon, I made yet another prediction that confirmed my reputation as a prophetess of airline disasters. I was appearing on a radio show in Tulsa, Oklahoma, when I spoke about another psychic dream I had had recently. In the dream, much like all the others, I had seen an American Airlines DC-10 crashing in Chicago. I was able to describe the location and even provide some details about the time when it would occur. I saw that this tragedy would come to pass within one month.

After the program ended we received many calls from listeners concerned for their safety and that of their loved ones. Chicago's O'Hare is the central airport for the Midwest, where a tremendous number of flights make stopovers during trips to other cities, so you can imagine how many listeners might have been planning a trip via Chicago within the month. I told those who called as much as I could about my dream, and—without frightening them—tried to encourage them not to travel by American Airlines for a while.

Four days later, I returned to the program and, trying to give a few more details about my vision, was able to come up with some numbers that I thought pertained to the doomed flight. Soon an American Airlines executive contacted me. As had happened before, the airlines people were concerned about my prediction and hoped to learn as much as possible. I told this executive everything I could, and we both hoped that the disaster could be averted.

Two weeks later I appeared on another radio program, this time I told listeners all I could about the crash, but unfortunately, had no new details to offer. A week later I appeared on another radio program in Cincinnati and again, I described my vision of impending death in Chicago.

One week after, almost exactly one month after my first dream, the DC-10 I had "seen" crashed in Chicago, killing many, and once again prompting stories describing my amazing powers. As with all my other major predictions of disaster, I was left in a state of terrible depression. At times, I would feel the way my mother and sister had before me: that I might somehow be *causing* these deaths and disasters. Fortunately, I was now mature enough to know that this is not so—and was able to dismiss these feelings of guilt before they overwhelmed me.

Number Nine: Grounding of the DC-10

Within a few short months I had yet another vision involving DC-10's. I was able to foresee that the DC-10 would be grounded in 1979, and that major structural defects would be discovered. I made this prediction in several newspapers, as well as in a newsletter I put out.

At first, when it became clear that my predictions had been accurate, I would wonder if a vision should have been able to prevent the disaster. In the past, however, not only my own predictions, but those of other famous and reputable psychics as well, had almost never been able to prevent disasters. And if *I* could not have prevented the tragedy, perhaps it would have been better if I had been spared yet another dream of pain and terror. But I cannot stop the visions.

My Last Important Prediction: The Middle East

The last prediction is really two separate ones that relate to a single issue: the recent crises in Iran and Afghanistan.

While the Shah was still in power, I predicted both his overthrow and the emergence of the Ayatollah Khomeini as Iran's revolutionary leader. At the same time, I was able to foresee Khomeini's illness and the heart trouble that would eventually require his hospitalization. Soon after that, I predicted a major confrontation between the United States and the Soviet Union in the Middle East over the area's rich oil fields. With Russia's invasion of Afghanistan, this prediction was proven accurate. I am so deeply concerned and involved with world politics that even though these predictions of trouble and turmoil may not seem as flamboyant as visions of death and disaster, they are of equal importance to me. I hope and pray that Frank Darling and other psychics like myself will be able to use our gifts to help America foresee the conflicts that arise all over the globe.

A Latter-Day Cassandra

It would seem as though someone with the ability to see into the future ought to be supremely self-confident and self-assured.

The exact opposite is true!

I am the most insecure person on the face of the earth. Torn by self-doubts, I am constantly calling my friends and family for reassurance. My gifts, my ability to predict, my second sight have all given me nothing but happiness—and insecurity. It is an ironic aspect of my inner honesty that I have had to face this fact.

Since childhood I have been haunted by the story of Cassandra, the accursed prophetess of ancient Troy. According to legend, her extraordinary beauty attracted the attentions of the god Apollo, who promised to bestow on her the spirit of prophecy if she would consent to be his bride.

After a prolonged courtship, Cassandra finally accepted his proposal, then—like many other young virgins—had second thoughts. Out of innocence and fear, she refused to share the marriage bed with her husband. And though Apollo could not revoke his supernatural gift, he took his revenge by turning his young bride's prophetic ability into a curse: From that time on, although her prophecies would continue to be accurate visions of the future, no one would believe a word she said. She correctly foretold all the important events in the world at large—the fall of Troy, her own rape by Ajax, the murder of Agamemnon—but her words fell on deaf ears, and she was unable to change the bloody history of her times.

I have been far luckier than that ancient princess; in small ways I have been able to help hundreds of friends and strangers foresee and cope with crises and dangers about to erupt in their lives. But all too often I have been powerless to prevent major tragedies that in my heart I have known were destined to occur.

Eyewitness to Tragedy

On December 27, 1976, my sleep was disrupted by a nightmare of incredible violence. I woke up in a fever, switched on the lamp, and entered the details of the dream in a notebook I always keep by my bedside just for that purpose. Two days later the nightmare occurred again, in every frightening detail. I can generally distinguish between a premonition and an ordinary dream by the intensity of the experience. And there was no doubt that this nightmare was a most extraordinary premonition. That what I'd seen kept recurring further convinced me that it was authentic and of singular importance. On January 2, during an interview on a New York radio station talk-show, I related this recurrent vision in these words: "I dreamt that I was on a 747 jet, on the runway of a tourist island thousands of miles from the United States. A mist was swirling on the ground."

I think the host was a bit taken aback by the anxiety in my voice. I took a sip of water, then continued.

"Suddenly, I saw the shadowy shape of another 747 bearing down on us. There was a fiery explosion as the other jet ripped into us."

As I write this, the images are still alarmingly vivid in my mind: the unearthly whine of the engines, the deafening shrieks of men and women surrounding me, the ocean of flames rolling over me. It was as if for one brief moment I occupied the body of one of the survivors—or one of the dead. I remember telling the host that "hundreds of bodies are strewn all over the airfield, like a grim battleground."

There was a commercial break, and the host pressed me for more details. I told him that one of the planes involved would be a Pan American jet, but that I couldn't be certain about the other plane. When we went back on the air I said to the host, "I have also been picking up images of a calendar opened to March."

Later, I heard that psychic Marsha Dixon (not her real name) of Miami had experienced a dream almost identical to mine—and apparently on the same evening that I first saw the two 747s collide. This uncanny coincidence was confirmation enough for me that a disaster of devastating proportions might occur sometime in March.

The day I made my prediction, Lila Preston (not her real name), a woman who operates a travel agency in New York City, was listening to the show. She was so concerned that she might book a client on the doomed flight that she called me the next day at home. "Which airlines will be involved?" she asked.

"One of the carriers will be Pan Am," I replied. "But I can't seem to form a clear impression of the other—although I have a feeling that it's a foreign plane." I repeated that the crash would occur at a tourist resort—and on the spur of the moment added, "Perhaps the Canary Islands."

In the succeeding weeks, I prayed that the dream would return once more, to let me pick up even just one more vivid detail—the flight number, the tail markings of the other jet, or the name of just one passenger on board. Several times I repeated my prediction for reporters and at public appearances. I was well aware that it was frighteningly specific, yet not specific enough.

As March approached, a black mood descended on me. I can't remember ever being as depressed. Above all, I was distressed by the feeling that even if I personally warned the pilots of the airplanes involved and exhorted every man, woman, and child scheduled to go on board to cancel their reservations, the tragedy would still happen. After a certain irreversible point, events seem to proceed with an inevitability of their own. Twice, psychic Jeane Dixon issued a warning that Senator Robert Kennedy would be assassinated in California in June of 1968. And Bobby bravely—but fatally—ignored her admonitions. In November of 1966, Irene Hughes predicted that "three men will die in a spaceship." And sixty-five days later a fire on board an Apollo capsule killed Gus Grissom, Edward White, and Roger Chaffee.

On May 21, 1969, Joseph DeLouise predicted that a jet plane would crash near Indianapolis, killing 79 people, and that number 330 would be important. On September 10, 1969, at 3:30 P.M., an Allegheny DC-9 collided in midair with a private plane over Indianapolis, killing the crew of 4 and 79 passengers. Over and over again, the leading psychics of our time have predicted catastrophes with phenomenal accuracy. But like Cassandra, they have been unable to prevent the tragedies they have foreseen.

The events of March 27, 1977, are a matter of record; the worst aircrash in history happened exactly as I had predicted: Two 747s were involved. One was a Pan Am jet, the other a foreign aircraft, and the crash took place on Tenerife, in the Canary Islands.

Could I have prevented the crash? Could I have issued some warning that I omitted? Have I somehow failed in my mission?

I shall never know. And these questions will haunt me until I die.

The Role of Psychic Research

Will a time come when people will pay more attention to the warning of psychics? In the future, will tragedies like that 747 crash be avoidable? I can understand the authorities' reticence to take bold action on the basis of one person's vision of the future. But shouldn't there be some way of using the knowledge that psychics command? When two or more psychics share a single vision, is that not reason enough to take action?

I would like to believe that in years to come, the advice and warnings psychics offer will be taken more seriously. The interest of governments and police departments in psychic phenomena leads me to assume that the role of the psychic is expanding rapidly—I wish only that these changes could happen quickly, before too many more lives are needlessly lost. But official acceptance of psychic phenomena requires scientific proof and a theory to support it. The majority of people are still nonbelievers, and they will not be easily convinced that someone like myself is able to see into the future. A convincing, strong body of evidence is needed to prove that psychic powers exist *and* can be utilized for the benefit of society. More testing and research will have to be undertaken, and large sums of money will have to be spent.

I myself have undergone tests and have been examined several times. Some of these tests have involved hypnosis, others have utilized certain drugs—of which I do not really approve. But the test results have helped me achieve a better understanding of my own powers. And before psychics can achieve acceptance as respected, legitimate authorities, more of these tests will have to take place.

Before this situation will improve, an accurate, concise explanation of psychic phenomena will have to be found. The legitimate psychic needs to be separated from the faker and the showman, and the psychic experience has to be distinguished from the elements of witchcraft and magic with which it is so often linked.

Perhaps the psychic is able to use some of the brain powers not used by most human beings. It may be through using heightened mental powers that he or she can predict the future.

In my approach to psychic phenomena, I try to be as scientific as possible, for unlike most psychics I know, I am very interested in research and testing. I like to keep accurate records of my predictions and find the percentage that turn out to be accurate.

In the meantime, however, I believe that our role as psychics will remain just about the same as it is today. From time to time we will be used by the police and by the government, but in a last-option capacity, after all other methods have failed. And we will be consulted most often by private individuals who believe in our ability to help them cope with their lives.

11
Giving Personal Advice

The professional psychic's life-style is a very unusual one. In some ways I have more freedom than most people. Not limited by strict work schedules or deadlines, I am free to set my appointments for whenever I choose, and if I want a day off to relax and think, I simply take one. On the other hand, I sometimes feel more trapped than most people do because I can never get away from my work. I cannot take off for a weekend and leave everything behind me, or go home from the office and put the day's business out of my mind—wherever I go and whatever I do, my visions and feelings follow me.

In some ways it is a very lonely life, yet I have actually come to love the seclusion and isolation. In fact, I need it in order to function as a psychic: If I cannot get enough time on my own to just sit and think, away from the constant drone of mental images and impressions that come to me from everyone I meet, I soon find my powers diminishing.

In this way, a crowded room can torture a psychic. No matter how hard I try to block things out, I am simply overwhelmed by messages and visions from those around me. If I let myself get exposed to too many people, I quickly begin to drown in their thoughts and problems, which are simply too much for me to take. So I try to keep to myself as much as possible. Lonely or not, I find it is the only way I can function.

On an average day I wake up between nine and ten o'clock in the morning—to some people this might seem like the good life, but you must remember that I tend to stay up very late at night. Every morning the first thing I do is listen to the news on the radio and read the morning papers. I'm not only an avid fan of current events, I also find it necessary for my work to keep up with what's happening in the world. Often a news item may lead me to some prediction of future events. And just staying in touch with the news helps me keep a fresh attitude about what's happening in our world.

At around eleven o'clock, I stop for something to eat. I'm a light eater, so I just have a small snack to give me mental energy. Heavy food, like red meat, has a tendency to detract from my powers of concentration. All my mental energy seems to focus on my stomach, and any sensitivity to my inner thoughts becomes impossible. So I prefer to eat light food such as fish, chicken, or vegetables. I'm also very concerned about nutrition, feeling as I do that mental fitness is directly related to the condition of your body. I watch what I eat, trying always to get the freshest and most natural foods, and I take vitamins to be sure I get all the nutrients I need.

As the afternoon begins, I can feel my psychic powers beginning to get stronger. Visions and feelings start coming to me, slowly at first, and then faster and faster as the day wears on. If I can, I like to get out of the house and walk around at this time of day. I live in Manhattan, not far from the East River, and I enjoy walking to the waterside to watch the movement of the tides. I find the effect of the water to be very soothing, and that helps me get more closely in touch with my inner mind. There is something mystical about the water—its quiet yet powerful motion, the vastness of the seas, and the interconnection of each drop with all the rest of the water on earth. Just gazing at the river or the sea tremendously heightens my psychic awareness.

Since I determine my daily schedule, it is easy for me to arrange time for these little excursions into my inner self. And although to others it may seem as though I'm wasting time while the rest of the world is working, relaxation is a vital part of my work.

Without the right mental environment, my gift cannot function at its peak.

From midafternoon until early evening I see clients at my apartment. As a professional psychic, one of my major activities is giving personal readings. Just as someone goes to a doctor's office for information or advice about their health, clients come to my home seeking answers too. The reasons they come are numerous, and the answers they find also vary constantly: Sometimes there is good news, predicting success or happiness; other times there are sad messages of illness, misfortune, even death.

Stars and Celebrities

As the years have passed, my reputation has grown, and well-known stars and celebrities have often asked me for readings about their careers and private lives: For several reasons, I have decided to refuse.

First of all, I believe that celebrities' lives change too quickly for my predictions to be helpful. When a person's life brings him to different parts of the world, constantly meeting new people and taking new jobs, it is very difficult for any psychic to predict future events for him or her with any degree of accuracy or certainty. But even more important, I just don't feel that I should be giving readings to stars and celebrities. This is something that's hard to explain, but I have the feeling that it is not right for me—that nothing I could say to a star would be of any real help.

It may seem as though I've made this decision without any real information, simply acting on the basis of feelings and intuitions—but after all, that's what my career is all about. Everything I do, every bit of information I give, is really an intuition. These feelings and hunches I get are the strongest tools I have, and if I don't pay attention to them, I am lost.

So when I have a certain compelling urge to do one thing and not another, I follow it. Nine times out of ten these urges are more accurate than many of the so-called facts I am told. I've made a career out of following my intuition, and I've helped lots of other people's careers in the same way. So when my feelings tell me not to become involved in reading for Hollywood stars, I listen. But even without famous (and probably high-paying) customers, I've done well for myself, and without charging outrageous fees—just enough to keep me going, and ensure that I won't have to read for more people than I can handle.

Sometimes I am asked if it's not dangerous to let strangers into my apartment for readings. The answer is no, because for the most part my clients are not strangers. In nine cases out of ten they are recommended to me by someone I know or have been consulted by in the past. And I always make a point of talking to the client on the telephone first. This way, before I meet them in person, I get a strong sense of who they are and what advice they are seeking. This is usually not enough of an impression from which to give accurate predictions, but it is a good way to weed out undesirable visitors.

Pranksters and Rip-Offs

Sometimes when a client calls to arrange for an appointment, I can pick up a strong negative feeling over the telephone. Somehow I just know they are not really interested in my professional services. Perhaps they do not really believe in my powers or in the existence of ESP. Or I may sense that a particular client is playing some kind of game—trying to test my abilities, hoping to trap me into making a false prediction to settle some bet or argument. I have better things to do with my time than be consulted by nonbelievers! People looking for proof of my powers must ask those I have helped in the past.

If someone chooses not to believe in psychic phenomena, that is fine with me and not my problem; I am not here to prove anthing to anybody. And I certainly cannot waste my time with pranksters or practical jokers. If anyone reading this has considered trying to stage such a spoof, they ought to forget it.

Psychic Groupies and Charlatans

There is only one other kind of client to whom I absolutely refuse to give advice—the people who seem to make a hobby of seeking psychic advice. They tend to be enamored of the whole world of parapsychology, telepathy, and the occult. Often they believe in witches and ghosts, and have consulted religious healers and mystics and lived in various communes. And some of them have come to me after consulting with five astrologers, seven palm readers, and numerous other psychics.

Only a short time ago a client visited me after she had already asked the very same questions of *fifty* other psychics! As a result, she was certainly the most confusing subject I have ever tried to read. Her head was absolutely crammed with various visions and impressions, each from a different psychic, and some so completely opposite in nature that it felt like trying to read fifty clients instead of one. I sent her home immediately, telling her that this was not a game. Psychic phenomena should not be a hobby or casual pastime, and overconsultation is an abuse.

Just one overly nervous or uncomfortable client can reverse the mood I've spent all morning working up. When a client is nervous, I am too. If their palms sweat, so do mine. I cannot keep myself from picking up the client's mood and feeling, so I do everything in my power to keep him as well as myself relaxed and at ease.

First Relax, Then Listen

When clients come to my home for personal consultation, I first try to get them to relax. During these sessions I try to create a quiet, comfortable atmosphere. I offer them a glass of wine. This usually puts my clients into a relaxed mood, and this kind of silent concentration is essential to the prediction process. Then I ask them to sit down. I've got a wonderfully comfortable chair I acquired specifically for clients to use. Once the client begins to feel at ease and once any initial nervousness or distress has subsided, the session can begin.

Before making any predictions, I try to talk with the client as much as possible. At times of course, I have an instant vision concerning a person the minute he or she walks in the door. But usually it helps to get to know clients a bit, to learn what is troubling them and what has motivated them to come to me.

A psychic will study a photograph or an object till visions begin to emerge. In the same way, it is useful for me to look at my clients, to listen to them talk. Then slowly, over several minutes' time, I begin to get feelings and images about them, and invite them to ask me questions.

The questions themselves, of course, help point me directly toward whatever area clients are concerned about. But just as important, I learn a great deal about clients by listening to the *type* of questions they ask. What interests them is very revealing of their character and personality.

Clients' questions are as limitless as are people's interests, problems, and imaginations, but generally they fall into a few basic categories. Love, naturally, is a major topic. People ask "Should I marry this person?" or "Is my husband going to leave me?" or "Does he love me truly?" They ask many questions about children, fertility, about when will they find the perfect lover. The second biggest area of inquiry is business. Everyone wants to find out how to make more money. Some come to ask if a certain business deal or investment will work out, and I am asked many career questions: "Am I on the right track?" "Should I change jobs?" and so on.

The third category—quite general and very broad—consists of inquiries about people's overall direction in life and in specific situations. They may be concerned about problems they are having with someone, or they may be wondering if their future lives will take a dramatic new turn.

My answers are almost always a direct response to the questions. Sometimes I cannot give an answer because I see no images relating to that particular inquiry. But in general, whatever the area—love, business, general direction, particular situations—I try to give the clients information they can use for *practical* purposes, to make their life better.

No News Is Bad News

One request that never ceases to amaze me is "Oh, don't tell me anything bad! I don't want to know about it!" Why would someone who isn't seeking the truth come to me in the first place? It is my policy to tell the client absolutely everything I can, regardless of whether or not it is pleasant to hear.

You see, I believe that almost nothing is final in this life. In the great majority of cases, something can be done. When I perceive serious—even fatal—illness in a client who believes himself to be healthy, I feel I must tell him or her about it. I believe it would be immoral to withhold such information just in order not to upset the client. Whatever the news, I want to share it.

Recently, for instance, a young woman came to ask about her near future. I had a strong impression that her grandmother was dying. I urged the girl to go to her grandmother immediately, for this might be her last chance to visit her alive. Convinced of my sincerity, the girl went to her grandmother's home. Unhappily, my prediction came true within days. But the girl later called and thanked me for helping her to make this one last visit possible. Whether or not it brings happiness, you see, I feel that knowledge is useful. Generally I give clients as much information as I can about the near future—up to one year from the time of our session. To me, this ability is a grave responsibility. My clients come to me for help, and are, in essence, placing their lives in my hands. So I must be as certain as possible that my advice is correct, and also that the client understands it properly.

The people who come to me have a deep belief in my powers, but I try to remind them that no one can be one hundred percent correct.

My rate of success tends to be about eighty percent, or at times even one hundred percent. The general tone and content of my visions will almost always be accurate, but only one in ten of the predictions I make for a client may come to pass *exactly* as I foresee.

Thus I feel a great responsibility to be as sure as possible before I make a prediction. If I could not feel sure and certain about my abilities, I would be in another business.

In fact, the percentage of my accurate predictions can be rather frightening to some people. In 1969, for example, I predicted the Arab oil embargo of 1973, and even the current Iran-Afghanistan crisis of the eighties. And many of the personal readings I give can be just as alarming as my visions of disaster or of business prospects.

From Business to Health

A few years ago, for example, a gentleman came to me for a personal reading. After we talked for a few minutes, he told me that he was interested in the future of a new business he was planning to invest in. We talked at length about the business, the amount he planned to invest, his feelings about the clients and partners involved. But as hard as I tried to concentrate, I could not get any image of this man's business life. All I could think about was his health.

When he had finished talking and was awaiting my response, I tried again to focus in on his investment—but without success. Finally I admitted that I could not give him any advice about the business and would not charge him for this consultation.

Then suddenly the vision became crystal clear: Something told me that this man had diabetes and was close to death. This image was so powerul that I knew I was obliged to tell him, even though he had not asked me.

Apparently he believed deeply in my power—or perhaps he was just impressed by the concern I was showing—but he went immediately to a doctor to seek professional medical advice. I always recommend that my clients visit a reputable doctor concerning health problems. I never attempt to give any medical advice myself, nor do I subscribe to any form of mystical healing or strange medical practices. I put my money behind the AMA!

Well, my vision of diabetes was correct. The man had been suffering for quite some time without knowing about it, and indeed was not far from death. Fortunately the doctors were able to stabilize his condition, and although he is diabetic, he is alive today. That client, by the way, created some lovely works of oriental art for me which hang in a place of honor in my home.

After a prediction like that, I feel good about having

helped someone who needed me, and am further convinced of the need to tell each client everything I can.

Sometimes I may spend an afternoon consulting a few truly fascinating clients—I take delight in meeting them, listening to them, and helping them. Either because of their personalities, or because of the nature of the visions they inspire, the sessions are exciting, vibrant, and joyful.

Other clients can be a bit boring. There's a constant parade of people who do *not* seek answers to life's problems, who do *not* want advice about their actions in the immediate future. Instead, they simply want to know when they will die!

Often people ask what has been the most unusual request ever made by a client consulting me for personal advice. The answer would lie with a man who came to my office about a year ago. We talked for a little while, and I sensed that he was a bit hesitant to come to the point. Then finally he asked me to go to bed with him! I thanked him, but declined—and did not take a rain check!

A Prophetess of Profit

The funniest, the most amusing client I ever had? My mother recently telephoned me about a household employee, a woman who works for one of my mother's neighbors and who wanted to meet me for some personal advice.

I told my mother I would be delighted to see her, and within a few days the woman arrived at my door.

She was middle-aged, wearing an old cloth coat that had been patched together in several places. Her simple clothing, rough hands and face suggested that she had been a manual laborer all her life. She had taken the bus and subway all the way from Queens to Manhattan, and she seemed tired and ready for a good night's sleep. She was very pleasant and friendly, but had played the servant for so long that she was a little uncomfortable about being treated as a guest in my house. She sat in my living room, refusing the glass of wine that I customarily offer my clients. My cat, Kisser, soon perched herself on the woman's lap, and immediately I sensed this woman's closeness with animals and children.

Strangely enough, she did not want to ask any questions about her personal life; instead, she wondered if our meeting had brought any numbers into my mind.

After I thought about this for a while, a number did come to my mind. As soon as I told it to my client, she got up and quickly left my apartment. A few days later, she reappeared—this time wearing a new cloth coat much nicer than her old one, and a new dress as well. We sat and talked, and still she was interested in numbers only. I concentrated, told her the number that came to my mind, and again she departed hastily for Queens.

When she arrived for her third visit she was wearing a fur coat, new shoes, and a fancy dress, but was concerned only to hear a number. And as soon as I told her the figures I "saw," she again left in a hurry. But this time, rather than going in the direction of the subway to Queens, she took a cab.

Within a few days she telephoned for yet another appointment. I told her that I would be happy to see her, but was admittedly confused about what she wanted to learn. She hadn't asked me for any personal advice, and didn't seem the least interested in getting any. "How can a bunch of numbers be of any possible use to you?" I asked her.

"Don't worry," she replied, after having described the new Cadillac she would be arriving in. "They are doing just fine. I've never been so lucky in my life!" Perhaps I should advertise myself not as a psychic, but as a professional gambling consultant!

Do clients ever request information or assistance that sounds unethical or immoral? For example, do people ever come to me looking for ways to cheat their business partners or swing a consumer rip-off? Honestly, this just doesn't seem to happen. I have yet to be consulted by a client whose questions do not concern something of vital and legitimate importance. And as long as the issue really does affect their lives, I am willing to help.

If clients are seeking business advice, for example, as a rule I do try to help them because success will improve their lives. I do not help people hurt anyone else, however. The very nature of my advice prevents this from happening.

Recently, I gave some advice to a client who was looking for a good investment for his money. Since he lives in Iowa, he was particularly interested in farming or livestock investments. I recommended that he buy thoroughbred racehorses, and I even suggested to him a few names of horses which just popped into my mind.

On returning to Iowa, he began to shop around for horses and soon found a few that bore the names I had given him, and others that were very similar to those I had "seen." As it turned out, he sold some of the horses for a fine profit, and races others himself for even more money. And he is now breeding horses in stables on his own farm.

Good Advice Goes Bad

Recently another businessman came to me who was also seeking a good investment for his savings. We discussed his interests and activities, and after a short while I received a vision concerning a warehouse. Above the warehouse door was a sign displaying the name of the company. When I mentioned the name to my client, he reacted with shock—it seems that a business friend had offered him some stock in that very company the day before!

I told him that he should buy that warehouse stock as quickly as possible. The stock would fluctuate for a while, and then shoot up to three times the price he paid. But I gave him some words of caution: "Once the stock has tripled, you should sell it immediately. To wait any longer will be dangerous."

In a few months my client had purchased that very stock, and its value was indeed climbing every day. Soon it was going for three times the price my client had paid. At this point, unfortunately, my client decided to ignore the warning I had given him and continued to hold out, hoping the stock would continue to rise.

Instead, within a few days the business papers reported a scandal among the company's management. Apparently there had been some illegal doings in the front office, and the price of the stock dropped dramatically that first day. Try as he might, the client could find no one to take the stock off his hands. Its problems had been too well publicized for anyone to be unaware of them.

Well, the client wound up losing his investment because he chose to wait for those few extra pennies. Although I can give people good advice, I can't force them to follow it!

My Biggest Mistake

I'm also sometimes asked about the mistakes I've made when giving psychic advice. This is quite an easy question to answer. I once made a prediction for great happiness, one that was even verified by another psychic—and, unfortunately, it didn't work out that way.

One day in March, a young girl I'll call Barbara had come to me with no specific problem to discuss; she simply wanted some indication what might happen to her in the next year.

As I talked to her, I got a very good feeling from her. I sensed that Barbara was a loving, tender, and considerate person. But she did seem a little unhappy with her present life-style. When I asked her about this, she admitted that although she was happy with her life, she was hoping it would improve within the next year. She was longing for a promotion at work and a new and better place to live. Of course any new home would depend upon the extra earnings that would come with a promotion.

I sensed that what she hoped for was going to happen; in fact, I suddenly envisioned the pages of a calendar turned to the month of May. I told her that great things would happen for her in that month. Then the vision grew even stronger. I told her that everything she longed for would come true on the twelfth of May. As you can imagine, she was delighted.

After our meeting, Barbara went to another psychic and told him what I had predicted. After a little conversation, he agreed with my feelings. He also sensed the twelfth day of May as being some turning point in her life and, just as I had, he assumed that that day would bring wonderful things.

As that fateful day approached, Barbara's feelings of anticipation became overwhelming, she was convinced (just as I and that other psychic were) that this was going to be the biggest day of her life. On the morning of the twelfth, before going to work, Barbara put on her very best clothes. She wanted to look great when that surprise check or promotion arrived.

She left the house just as she had every other morning, and headed down into the subway, looking her very best.

Well, she was mugged when she went down into the subway. She wasn't injured, but her purse and money were taken and she was badly shaken up. In the scuffle, one of her shoes fell off, landed on the tracks, and was run over by an oncoming train. She broke the heel of her remaining shoe leaving the subway.

And once Barbara got to work that morning, things continued to go from bad to worse—she was fired! Clearly, Barbara's big day was not working out quite as planned.

With nothing else to do, she returned home. When she entered her apartment, she saw a small piece of paper on the floor. Some kind of legal document had been slipped under the door. It was an eviction notice.

On May 12 Barbara had been mugged, fired, and evicted—all within two hours' time. This was unmistakably the most incorrect prediction I have ever made! Although May 12 was an important day, my signals were badly crossed. But as it turned out, the effect of that day on Barbara's life was all to the good. She ended up moving to a different part of town, where she found a much nicer apartment for about the same rent. And she soon found another job that she enjoyed more—and which paid her a better salary.

Most important of all, at this new job she met a man with whom she fell in love; they are now planning to be married. So I suppose that my prediction for that day did finally come true indirectly. But I still think that piece of personal advice was one of the biggest mistakes I ever made.

Sometimes, after a prediction like this one, I will question my abilities. At times I even hesitate to meet with more clients until I have reconsidered my accuracy as a professional psychic. I'm not afraid of failure. I have learned to accept false predictions and not to be too hard on myself about them.

But I think it is only natural that I am temporarily upset by mistakes like the one involving Barbara. Try to imagine yourself performing some function at work—something you do every day and pride yourself on being good at—only to discover afterward that you'd done the job all wrong, making a terrible mistake at something you thought you knew well. For a short time, at least, you would naturally feel a little insecurity and self-doubt.

12
A Gift Regained

When I finally made the move and committed myself to the psychic life, Maria was a great help to me. And yet in our conversations she often spoke about eventually leaving me. She would say that each day I would need her help less and less.

But there were periods of a week or so when no clients came at all. These times gave me an opportunity to relax and think, but certainly didn't help pay the bills. And there were setbacks, afternoons—just as there still are today—when a client would come to ask a question, and try as I might, my powers wouldn't work. I always refused to accept any payment in these cases, since I felt I really hadn't helped at all.

The Statue in the Box

After I had been in professional practice for several years, something very unusual happened to me. To this day I cannot explain why I suddenly found myself unable to give readings. Week after week, try as I might, I could not make any predictions.

This feeling was very confusing and troubling. I felt separated from my own powers, from my very self. Never before in my life, not even when I had been a little girl, had I ever felt my gift slipping away. No amount of denial or suppression had ever been able to halt my visions, and now they had stopped on their own!

Over and over again I repeated the prayer Maria had taught me: "With the infinite good that is in me, I pray to the infinite good that is within you, dear God..."

But still I was unable to make my gift return. During the first few days I sensed that my powers were trapped inside me, trying to get out, but blocked by some strange force. After more time passed, I lost even that slight sensation of lingering power, and began to fear that my gift was slipping away forever.

In desperate fear, I called Maria. Naturally she told me to come see her at once. Back in her charming apartment once again, I sat down on her living room couch.

"You feel your power drifting away, Shawn."

I nodded and began to cry bitter tears.

"But the gift can *never* leave you. It is strong and healthy. But you have locked it up inside."

"How?" I asked. "It's been years since I tried to suppress my powers."

"When I was your age," Maria softly replied, "I had just begun my professional career. Things were going fine. I was building a reputation, a clientele. My life was moving steadily forward. But then, one odd day, my gift just seemed to dry up like an old well with no water left within it. I could not understand this. Just like you, I had done nothing *consciously* to block my powers. And yet something within me was holding them back. Something was preventing my conscious mind from listening to my inner thoughts and visions."

As I listened to her tale, the tears slowed. She got up from the couch and crossed the room to an antique cabinet.

"Without knowing it, I had closed the door to my inner mind. And behind that door, my visions were trapped." She reached into the closet and took out a lovely hand-carved wooden box. "And the strangest thing about this problem was that it disappeared as mysteriously as it came. I did not know where it came from, and I did not know why it went away. But what made the change occur was something my teacher told me."

She carried the box over the couch and sat down beside me. On the front of the box was a little wooden door with a tiny handle.

"She said something to me—a simple, ordinary phrase people use every day. But when she used it, my powers returned." She handed the box to me. "The phrase, Shawn, was 'Open the door.' "

I looked at the wooden box.

"Open the door, Shawn."

I did, and inside the box was a small statue of Buddha.

"The door has been opened now, Shawn. Take the statue with you and keep it forever. The door will never close again."

I brought the statue home to my apartment, and from that day on, my powers have never deserted me. In fact, they have only grown stronger and stronger. And with that little statue of Buddha began my interest in Eastern religions and philosophy. My reading about and study of these schools of thought have brought me tremendous revelations into the meaning of life and of my own powers.

Maria Takes Her Leave

After that meeting I again began to feel Maria's presence moving away from me. During our rare conversations she constantly mentioned my decreasing need of her help.

I now realize what she was foreseeing. In 1978, on Thanksgiving Day, I went to my parents' house in Queens. My sister came to visit with her husband and two children, and we had a lovely afternoon together talking about the years gone by.

We all sat down to dinner and gazed at the array of dishes, vegetables, sweet potatoes, and dressing. My father was carving the turkey when my mind suddenly began drifting away from the people around me. Then I could see Maria lying in her apartment. She looked quiet and peaceful as she glanced at me. "Good-bye, Shawn," she said. "You are now ready for the life that lies ahead of you. My work with you is done. But remember: Never stop saying your prayer. I love you. Good-bye. . . ."

At that instant I knew that Maria was dead. And suddenly I felt a surge of power running through me, as though my gift had grown three times stronger than before. Now, after her death,

Maria's presence surrounded me more than it had since we had first met one another. In that moment she had passed her powers along to me.

Since that day, I have missed her sorely, and yet I know that her loving support and kindness will remain with me all my days. And probably, someday soon, there will be another young girl just like I used to be who will need a teacher, a "psychic mother," a friend. And it will be my job to help her just as Maria helped me.

Among professional psychics there's a real temptation to have office hours running from morning till night in order to generate as much business as possible. But if I try to read for too many people in a single day, I don't think any of them end up getting a really clear and accurate reading. It's just too much for me. Although I can control my gift and "call up" visions when I try, I just can't do so twenty times a day.

"Calling Up" Visions

With time and experience, I think I have matured enough to handle almost every vision that comes to me. Like any talent or ability, psychic powers are developed and molded.

After enough work and struggle one eventually comes to gain some control. Whereas my dreams are completely unexpected and beyond my control, many of my waking visions are "called up," so to speak. And I exercise this same kind of control over my gift when I work for the police. When asked to help find a criminal, for instance, it would be useless to simply let my mind wander. It is far more likely that I will find a clue by directing my attention to the objects, or vibrations, at the scene of the crime.

When I consult with a client, I have the ability to make visions happen. By concentrating and directing my thoughts, I can focus in on the subject's problems. These visions are really quite simple and painless. Someone might come to me, for example, seeking personal advice and at one point in our conversation I may suddenly have a clear vision of a certain date.

In a case like this, I tell the client to watch out for a special event on that day—something important will happen then, and he or she should be prepared to act. Or a man may ask me if he should marry a certain young lady. Many times I can simply answer no or yes on the basis of the emotional vibrations I receive from the client. Of all the types of predictions I make, these seem the easiest.

With still other readings, I simply get an image of the client in a particular place, or performing a certain task. By combining this image with what I learn about the client, I can give some accurate information about the future. For instance, if a young man asks me what career he should choose, I first try to learn as much about him as I can. Let's suppose he tells me that he enjoys both scientific studies and working with his hands. During our session, if I get a quick impression of him working in a medical clinic, I will tell him that I see him working at a medical clinic in the future. So far, I've been right about eighty percent of the time.

During my consultations the visions often seem to come easily, but I have a difficult time remembering these perceptions. It is as though I am in a completely altered state of consciousness; as if I have left my body and my surroundings for a short while and am somewhere outside the real world. It is not uncommon for me to make several predictions for a client, only to forget them a few minutes alter. To prevent this, I make as many notes as possible.

In a way, I suppose this whole process of seeing the future is not unlike going into a trance. Sometimes I truly feel as though I have been transported away from reality; at other times just a quick, powerful thought pops into my mind.

Many of my visions and predictions come to me as I am doing other things. I can be reading a book or listening to music when a vision comes to me. Sometimes they even occur while I am in the middle of a conversation.

Since I never know when a vision will come, I must pay close attention to all my thoughts and feelings every day of my life. For I have no way of knowing when a daydream might include a vital piece of information about the future.

When Will It Happen?

I'm often asked an interesting question: How can I tell when a particular event will happen? How does a vision express the time factor?

As I've said, every vision is unique; each new psychic experience has a completely distinctive feeling about it. Whether it is a particular color or the lighting or taste or scent, every vision distinguishes itself in some way from all the rest. Similarly, each vision expresses its time reference in a different way. Although it may sound like a shot from an old Hollywood film, in many visions I *do* see calendar pages. Sometimes a clock is dominant in the vision, often even illuminated so that it cannot be missed. In these and in other ways, some dreams—particularly those that happen involuntarily—are insistent about time reference. Someone or something wants me to be quite certain about when the vision will come to pass.

In other visions the time factor may be more hidden. I may see someone outdoors, and thereby be able to deduce the season of the year. Or the vision may show the subject sitting down to dinner, so that I can tell the hour of the day.

In still other visions the time factor is completely obscure. No references are given that would help me establish or even guess when the event will come true. But in most of these cases the client *himself* is able to find some time reference that I do not know about. For example, someone might come to me seeking business advice, and want to know if a big deal will come through and when to expect some result.

In my vision which I would probably "call up," I may see my client laughing and shaking hands with Mr. Smith. A signed contract lies on the desk before them, and the location is a large dining hall full of crystal chandeliers. From the vision I can deduce that my client and Mr. Smith will indeed come to an agreement on the business deal. But I have no definite time factor to refer to, and thus cannot answer the second half of my client's question.

But here is where the client can help himself. *He* may be able to recognize that fancy dining hall (which held no significance for me) as the place where he sees Mr. Smith once a month for a particular businessman's luncheon. The client can thereby deduce that the deal will be signed at that monthly luncheon. Many times elements of a vision make little sense to me, but have clear meaning for the client. And in such circumstances, the client's active participation is vital.

The process of making predictions is illogical and beyond complete scientific analysis at this time. The interpretation of visions, though, is largely a common sense situation. The psychic dreams and visions I have tend to be obvious, or at most, only slightly obscured. Long hours of consideration and theorizing are not required to make sense of them. They are not like normal dreams in which may be hidden secret feelings that only years of analysis could uncover. They are straightforward and simple to grasp (in the case of visions of disaster, all too painfully simple).

What *is* tricky is being able to tell whether predictions are real; though as far as I'm concerned, there is no difference: True and false predictions looks and feel the same, and both are definitely outside the realm of common dreams, passing thoughts, or even daydreams, being stronger and more immediate.

I suppose the majority of my predictions occur because I want them to. But there are times when for one reason or another I cannot get an image or feeling about a certain subject, no matter how hard I try. The exact reason for this kind of failure is hard to pinpoint. Perhaps my mood isn't correct, or it may be a question of body chemistry—I may be feeling poorly physically, or just may not have the energy needed to make a prediction.

Perhaps I was not intended to see some parts of the future. There may exist certain limitations on what can be seen. I do not pretend to understand the reasons for such cosmic secrecy, but sometimes I do get the impression that I may be searching for information I can never know.

But there are more logical reasons for my occasional failures. I think that to a great extent they have to do with the client's attitude. Often someone comes to me seeking advice on a problem when he or she is in fact feeling more bothered by another situation. At such times I often find myself answering questions that the client hasn't asked. But once in a while I simply come up blank—the client and I are not on the same wavelength, and nothing at all comes through.

These failures raise some very interesting questions. I find it easier to explain why my predictions have come true than to explain why they may be false. For when I am asked why a prophecy does come true, I can simply answer: "Because my powers work, and that's about it." But when the system fails, I am at a loss for a complete and satisfying explanation. Perhaps false predictions are actually true predictions that have somehow been avoided. For example, if I dreamed about a certain plane crashing and that plane was then grounded before takeoff, this wouldn't mean that my prediction was false. Rather, that tragedy would simply have been averted.

It may be hard to believe that the prediction of future events can contain any form of logical thought. But if you experience psychic phenomena as long as I have, you begin to understand the rhymes and reasons involved. And eventually certain patterns begin to emerge. During a vision, my body responds physically. I can feel the nerves tingle. Often I begin to perspire. Friends who have been with me say my eyes seem to dilate and grow larger.

The change in my body chemistry during such visions is one reason I believe physical health is necessary to sustain strong psychic powers. The entire process is very draining on the system. When I am sick, for example, I find it very difficult to get my visions to come—it seems that I am somehow out of tune with my body and therefore with my mind as well. Because of this connection between psychic power and good health, I try to do all I can to nourish myself properly. I also believe, however, that too much food is just as bad for the mind as too little.

Besides physical health, what else influences psychic powers? Relaxation is essential, of course. Without a calm, peaceful mood, I cannot think clearly or concentrate. And when I am not relaxed, the visions I have tend to be garbled and often impossible to interpret.

During the afternoon, I usually give readings to several

clients. Sometimes these sessions continue until seven or eight o'clock in the evening. After these appointments I am on my own again. Sometimes I dedicate the evening to study, at other times to pleasure. Both are extremely important aspects of my day's work. Whether I am going out with friends, or just sitting at home studying world affairs or reading about archaeology, I always try to improve my powers and abilities.

I have many methods for putting myself in the mood for my work. A bigger problem is handling the situation. Emotional strain, physical pressure, responsibility, and the sense of impending disaster can cause psychics a lot of anxiety.

And some psychics are unable to handle these pressures. Many well-known psychics have a tendency to drink too much, or to attempt to solve their problems through other damaging, draining means such as drugs. There are times when I feel that the pressure is too much, but at these times I am forced to remind myself of the importance of my work and my responsibility. What keeps me going is this sense that I am doing something that can benefit others.

Leisure Time

Without the opportunity to get away from the constant pressures of the psychic life-style, I wouldn't be able to work at all. The old adage about all work and no play is especially true for the professional psychic. Keeping calm, unhurried, and relaxed is absolutely essential to the day-to-day process of prediction.

I don't have any real hobbies—at least not as most people think of them. But several interests do form an important part of my life. These I do not pursue simply for fun, though, and so my leisure time is not unrelated to my work. Besides walking down to the river, whenever I can I try to get out of New York City and take a trip to the beach. Of course, I enjoy natural settings of any kind—forests, mountains, streams, or lakes are all delightful to the senses. But being by the sea is really something special. Just to stare out at the vastness of the ocean that stretches from one horizon to the other as far as the eye can see. . . I find it to be pure and total joy. I like to stroll along the shoreline for hours, collecting seashells and thinking. During these lazy hours it's amazing how many visions and images flow through my mind. At times the power I feel seems to increase, so much so that it actually surges through my body.

The other great delight of my leisure time is reading. I love to read, and I devour nonfiction books on virtually any topic, from politics to science to archaeology—almost any nonfiction subject appeals to my interests.

Many people send me books and news stories relating to psychic phenomena, assuming they will interest me; but in fact, they don't. I no longer study my chosen profession. Whereas earlier I spent hours—years—searching hungrily for books about any form of psychic phenomena, I now do not read anything on the topic at all. For me, the point of reading or relaxing is to get *away* from my business, to let my mind wander. By reading about almost any other aspect of life, I can lead my mind closer to visions and feelings and dreams of the future. But when I try to study the psychic process itself, I discover that for some reason my powers are weakened.

I have become very involved with the study of Zen Buddhism and other oriental religions. The teachings of the Zen Masters have given me a great deal of inspiration and comfort. I feel that meditation and self-examination is a perfect way to reach the kind of mental bliss that brings on the strongest psychic phenomena.

One of my unfulfilled desires in life is to visit the Himalayas. Although I sometimes feel that I am able to travel to these lands in my mind, I want very much to actually go there one day. I believe these people would understand my powers and could help me completely understand the questions that still trouble me to this day.

Another of my dreams involves joining an archaeological dig, searching among the ruins of an ancient civilization for clues about our past, as well as hints concerning our future. But most of all, I would like to find some relic of the past that would provide unqualified proof that there is indeed a God. For although I may not seem religious by common standards, I believe with all my heart in the existence and powers of one true God.

The one factor of my life-style that probably separates me from other people is my obsession with news events. I find myself reading several newspapers every day and listening to or watching as many news broadcasts as possible. Every week's mail brings so many magazines that I no longer have time to read them all through. Add to this the number of nonfiction books I read each week, and a pretty clear picture should emerge of how I spend most of my free time. I find that even some seemingly minor event—in the Mideast, for example— can lead me to a larger, more important vision of some major event that will not occur till perhaps ten or twenty years from now. Knowing what has happened in the world today is the best route to predicting what will occur tomorrow.

Ninety-nine Percent Logic, One Percent Psychic

In my opinion the study of psychic phenomena is closely related to psychology: The majority of psychic occurrences result from the *normal* functions of the human mind. For example, my personal readings are usually about ninety-nine percent logic and only one percent psychic. I make many of my predictions simply by listening to clients and by being sensitive to their moods and feelings. Once you understand an individual, predicting what may happen soon in their lives is largely a matter of common sense.

It is very possible that the remaining one percent of the process that *cannot* be explained as ordinary logic or reason may very well be a special, hidden power of the human mind. Rather than being a message from the great beyond, perhaps a vision is simply the result of activity in some part of the brain that in most people is usually inactive.

Psychologists are quick to admit that they do not yet completely understand how the brain functions. There are whole areas of the human brain whose activity experts cannot yet decipher. We are told that most of us utilize only a small portion of our brain—and no one can yet say with certainty what those unused portions are capable of.

Friends of All Ages

I try to keep myself calm, rested, and quiet. A few nights each week I like to go out to Japanese restaurants, for I find them particularly restful. There is a certain peaceful quality to all things Oriental. For me, music is another great sedative. With the right kind of music, I find myself easily slipping off into visions even before I know it is happening. But at other times I visit friends or visit quiet, out-of-the-way places where I can free my mind of outside images and just relax. For when I stand in a crowded place, I simply cannot fight off the influx of thoughts, feelings, and worries from those around me.

By most standards, my friends would be considered quite an unusual group. Many are older—some in their forties, others as old as seventy. Although they come from all types of backgrounds, most of them are involved in the arts. Whether musicians, painters, or writers, each of the individuals I am drawn to has a particular talent or creative gift. Because of the very close connection that I believe exists between psychic phenomena and creative ability, this is not really surprising.

What *is* surprising is that while these older friends all believe deeply in my gift (some even more so than I myself do!), all my younger friends are nonbelievers. Not that they dispute or doubt my own belief, they are just not particularly convinced of the legitimacy of the whole field of parapsychology.

That these younger friends are nonbelievers truly does not offend or upset me at all. They are wonderful, exciting human beings, and I treasure them as friends whether or not they accept my powers. In one respect, this skeptical attitude is quiet refreshing. From time to time, however, I have strong visions concerning these doubting friends. And although they don't put much stock in my predictions, I tell them anyway. You see, I would rather risk an incorrect vision than risk the potential tragedy and guilt of keeping to myself a true prediction of danger or unhappiness. It is far easier for me to tell what I "know," and let my friends, or anyone else, take whatever action they consider appropriate. Once I have stated what I feel to be true, my problem is over. People's reactions must be their own responsibility.

But often I have very difficult nights dominated by haunting and frightening visions that will not leave me alone. These are the times when I am very likely to foresee a tragedy or disaster.

These powerful and devastating dreams are beyond my control. I cannot prevent them, nor can I make them happen. And, as you might have guessed, these are far from pleasant evenings.

13
Dreams of Disaster

When a tragic vision is imminent, I find it difficult to rest or sleep until it occurs. Once the dream is past, I may feel upset and shaken but then I know that the dream was important and necessary, and I can sleep soundly once again.

Psychic dreams, to begin with, are very distinctive and different from common dreams. Normal dreams tend to be in color, last only a short while, and change quickly from one dream to the next. A psychic dream-vision, however, is never in color—at least mine aren't. Always in a shade of gray, very moody and subdued, they tend to be filled with mist, and give me the feeling that I am walking through some darkened, foggy land. No matter what the message of a particular dream might be, the main characteristics remain the same. The content may vary, but the elements of fog and heightened illumination are usually involved. The unique quality of psychic dreams, though, is that I always feel as if I am being led into them, as if something is being shown to me, rather like an educational film, so that I may learn something important. Something or someone else seems to be controlling what happens, while I am only there to learn. My visions—not the inventions of my imagination, nor the visualizations of my subconscious mind—seem to come from some outside source.

"Experiencing" a Disaster

The major elements of the dream always stand out clearly. If the dream concerns an automobile, for example, the car will be very visible in the fog. It will be almost illuminated, and is always easily recognizable.

Many of these dreams concern airline crashes and disasters, and in them I can always see the plane clearly. For a while I become a passenger on the plane as it goes up into the sky. I am very aware of the impending crash; I can feel the plane going down as the land comes closer and closer. When the crash finally occurs, I *feel* it. I experience all the pain the accident will cause and share the other passengers' terror, fear, and confusion.

And then I experience death: I feel myself passing through the barrier between this world and the next. Because this is so, many people ask me about life after death. But I cannot answer those questions. In these dreams, I do not actually learn what happens after death. I simply experience the moment when life is transcended. I think the dream includes this feeling of death so that I will know that the tragedy that I am foreseeing will be complete: People will be killed.

After experiencing the crash and the sense of death, I find myself stepping outside the tragedy. I am outside the plane, looking back at what remains of the machine and its passengers. I watch as emergency workers and medical people arrive. From looking at the bodies, I often get a distinct impression of who will be on the plane.

And there tends to be some other clue about what plane will crash and when—a flight number, name, date, time, or particular airport appears in the dream. Whatever the circumstances, the dream somehow gives me a clue so I can make use of what I have been shown.

The emotions I experience in dreams like this are very hard to handle. The sheer terror of knowing death is inevitable is probably more than most people could cope with. In fact, the process of having psychic visions is a dangerous one for emotionally unstable people. I believe many individuals have been born psychic, only to find that they could not live with the experience. It surprises people that despite the emotions I experience during some of my predictions, I do not fear them at all. When I was young, though, and lacked the experience to understand my visions, I very often found them frightening. But now that I know my ability's power and importance, I no longer fear the struggle involved. In a way, it is a relief to have dreams of tragedy. Perhaps that sounds a bit morbid, but keep in mind that these visions of tragedy and death are being sent to me because they are *lessons* I must learn, stories that must be told.

My job becomes easier with practice. I often feel that I am growing stronger with each passing day. Like a long-distance runner who feels as though she will surely die after her first marathon, only to go on to longer and longer races, the effort becomes less overwhelming with each try.

And yet there are still those dreams of terrible tragedy, where I sit in the fog and gloom among a hundred people crying out in terror and agony. I listen to the deafening scream of metal as we collide with the runway, and watch as bodies are dragged from the wreckage. These visions are no easier to accept than they were in my youth.

And I awake, frightened and shaken. I search my mind for steps I might take to prevent this horrible disaster from occurring. I run to the telephone and call the airlines, the aviation authorities, perhaps even someone I saw on the plane whom I can identify.

But no one pays much attention. And within a few days or weeks my vision of death has left my dreams and appeared on the front pages of newspapers.

"Just another coincidence," people will say. And just another day in the life of a professional psychic. It is, all in all, a strange and confusing process. On the one hand, the pain and horrible emotions bring relief once they have passed. On the other hand, the true pain comes later, when I try to convince people of the danger I have seen, and they refuse to believe me.

Would I—Could I—Change It All?

It's certainly easy to get the impression I am not very happy with my life. But the fact is, I love it and am actually very happy—or at least as happy as I can be. There is a great freedom that comes in facing a task and accomplishing it well, and a great sense of accomplishment in the knowledge that I am helping people.

If I could, what would I change about my life? Not one thing! I feel that I have had complete control of my life, except of course for the gift I have received. Beyond that, I have played the game exactly as I chose to—and so far, I'm winning.

I have done a great deal so far in life, and I intend to do much more. I have traveled the world, seen the cathedrals of Europe and the gambling tables of Las Vegas. Mine has not been a deprived existence.

Perhaps my life will be quite different one day, but that isn't how I see it. Through my powers, as well as through knowing myself, I "know" I will be leading a very similar life many years from now. By continuing to do everything I can to use my gift for good purposes I will, with luck, be able to help many, many people. But I'll be satisfied if I only manage to help even a few.

For me, the most important question—Is it all worth it?—leads me to pause and think about some of the people I have helped, whether it was aiding the police in solving a baffling crime, or in helping a personal client avoid injury or seek medical help for an undetected ailment. And then I quickly find the answer to my question: Yes, it is. Just knowing that I have perhaps saved one person's life makes my own worth living.

But if I wanted to go back and do it differently, could I change my life-style? How could I possibly erase the years of development of hard-won strength? How could I make the visions stop, the feelings go away? I simple cannot escape my own mind; I cannot get away from the truth of my life. And I don't even want to. There simply is no turning back. I've grown accustomed to this life of visions and dreams, have learned to accept the pain of foreseeing death, and I no longer fear the sadness these visions bring.

It is still a painful process in many ways, but even though bad news seems to arrive almost every day, I prepare for it by trying to remain optimistic. I simply remind myself of all the good I can do with my powers, and somehow the hard times seem easier.

I don't let sadness and fear harden me to the problems of others, and I don't see how I ever could grow so used to death and sadness that they cease to upset me. And no matter how bad things may seem, my curiosity keeps me going. Knowledge, even if it brings sadness, is too tempting to ignore. The kind that comes to me is especially tempting, and particularly hard to forget.

I'm still written up in newspapers and magazines quite often—more and more every year, in fact. And if you're reading this book, chances are you first saw my face on a page of the *Enquirer* at your local grocery store's checkout counter. I have been very happy with this newspaper, and I expect our relationship will last for some time.

Even now that I have attained recognition and business has become steady, for the last year or so my life has changed very little. Each day is pretty much like the one before it. I do the same things, go to the same places to relax, and see just about the same number of clients.

"Aunt Witch"

My sister Helene has been married for quite a while now to a wonderful man named Norman. Their two beautiful boys—Stephen, who is ten, and Seth, eight—give me a lot of joy. Stephen and Seth call me Aunt Witch, which can sometimes be quite embarrassing, especially when we're out in public. Both boys are very interested in my work, and never fail to point me out whenever they see me on the cover of a newspaper at the grocery store. They are very proud of my "celebrity" status, and take some pleasure in bragging about me.

And although my sister stopped pursuing her psychic abilities long ago, she now finds herself the mother of two very gifted boys. Stephen has already begun to show signs of great powers. Several days before the tragic DC-10 crash in Chicago, for example, he told me that he had dreamed that just such an accident would occur in that city within a few days.

So although Helene may have suppressed her own power successfully, she could not prevent herself from being a genetic carrier of psychic ability, and has passed this power on to her children.

As for romance, I don't really have a love life. My continuing warm relationship with Frank Darling gives me great satisfaction and happiness. I no longer seek new romantic relationships or go out on dates as they are traditionally defined. And I do not see myself forming any new romantic alliances in the future. I simply do not believe that that is where my life is headed.

Perhaps the reason is that I feel I cannot handle my career's demands and still function as a competent and loving wife and mother. I'm really not sure. Of course there are times when I fantasize about having a family of my own, but my own predictions for myself tell me that this will never happen. It just doesn't seem fair to bring children into the world when I do not think I could provide the kind of love, care, and attention that a child depends on. My dreams and visions would forever be dragging me back to my profession. At this point I cannot expect to turn my life around and choose such a completely different direction. I would enjoy being a mother; in fact, I believe it is one of the highest callings on this earth. It is simply that I have a certain job to do—one I never asked for, but have been given anyway—and I cannot walk away from it; I don't think it would be possible, nor would it be right.

In a way, I am like a member of the clergy: I feel I have a calling I must answer to do God's work. I am certainly not bored; on the contrary, I'm now what I always wanted to be: calm, relaxed, and dedicated to my work and study. And if something is just the way you want, why try to change it? I don't believe in fooling around with a good thing. I'm happy, and plan to stay that way. In fact, I *know* I will!

I can almost picture myself sitting in my apartment thirty or forty years from now. I will have just finished my walk to the river and will be awaiting the arrival of my first client of the day. It will be a different world then; many things will have changed. But the questions I am asked will never change too much. I will still be telling people about great investments, about big days to come, about that perfect lover they will meet, and about how many *C*'s their kids will get in college.

It's a strange life I lead, painful but good. Perhaps I am painting a rather gloomy picture of the psychic life, but I am doing what I can to change this: This book is part of my effort. But until the rest of our society decides to examine the facts, to separate those of us who practice fraud or trickery from those who are legitimate, until then the future *will* be fixed and unchangeable.

But it doesn't have to be. Together we can change the future. We have the power, and I suggest we use it now.

Part Three

Changing Your Own Future

14
How Psychic Are You?

Interest in psychic phenomena has grown tremendously over the past several years. From a time when ESP and precognition were considered sideshow tricks, we've come into an age when police departments saddled with baffling cases are willing to consult psychics. If the police are willing to admit that some psychics are possibly legitimate, then we must be doing something right.

More and more people come to me suspecting that they may have some psychic powers. And they are troubled, fear being different from everyone else, and are especially worried about "knowing" of the death and tragedy around them. I understand these feelings completely. But the psychic powers most people are likely to have need not be feared. On the contrary, they can be a help in daily life.

Know Your Psychic!

What most angers me about the world of psychic phenomena is the group of con artists and fakers who have turned at least part of it into a cheap industry. So many of these charlatans, as they might be called, who read palms and tea leaves and hand out flyers on the street, also lie and cheat. The problem is, the people whom they take advantage of cannot afford to spend their lives' savings on bad advice—old poor people who go back to the same charlatan over and over again, some fake who keeps telling them that they have been cursed and can escape certain doom only by giving all their money to the "psychic."

Recently, in New York, a woman actually killed her infant child because such a "seer" had told her that the poor baby was possessed by the devil and was in need of purification. There is no limit to the damage such people can do. As long as there are desperate people willing to believe anyone who claims to be able to help, these parasites will continue to get rich off the sufferings of others. The only way to put these people out of business is to stop seeing them. If you or anyone you know is in the habit of supporting these criminals, stop seeing them immediately. They cannot help; they can only harm.

By way of advice, I suggest that before you consult any psychic you learn as much as you can about him or her. Try to find friends or associates who can recommend you to someone they have seen in the past and trust implicitly. Since there really is no rating system for psychics, this kind of personal testimonial is about your best available guarantee.

Trust That Intuition!

Everyone has some psychic power. We usually call it intuition, though most people underestimate how powerful it is. Have you ever said to yourself, "I know I shouldn't have said that," or "Something told me not to buy this car"? You had a psychic experience without even realizing it. That nagging feeling inside you, warning you not to say or do something, is your natural intuition at work. Had you chosen to listen, you might have been able to avoid some trouble. But most people pay absolutely no attention to their own hunches and expectations. We have all been conditioned, it seems, to accept what others advise or promise, rather than put a little more faith in ourselves.

It's hard to say where this determination not to trust ourselves comes from. Perhaps it is very natural, in a way, to assume that you know less than the next fellow, or that he has some information you don't. But when does this cautious feeling of doubt become an obsessive bad habit?

Think of all the advice your subconscious mind offers you each day that you choose to refuse instead! Whenever you suspect that someone you are dealing with cannot be trusted, you are having a psychic experience. Whenever you wake in the morning with a feeling that a certain event you planned will not take place, you are having a psychic experience. Whenever you answer the phone and feel you *knew* that person would call, you are having a psychic experience. Every time a mother senses her child may be in trouble, she is having a psychic experience.

It happens to everyone, almost every single day. And yet we consistently ignore our intuitions; instead of using them to guide and direct our activities, they simply go to waste. There are several simple steps you can take to start making use of what you feel instead of ignoring it. The first is to tell yourself: "I have psychic power." It's an easy thing to say, but a hard thing to convince yourself of.

Testing Yourself

It may take a long time to start believing that you could actually be psychic. So in the meantime, provide yourself with a little experiment. If it convinces you of the need to follow your intuition, it will have been worth your while.

For the next few days pay close attention to any nagging suspicions and doubts. Try to keep track of the times that you follow your feelings *and* the times you ignore them. For example, if you are shopping for a small appliance, and you find a salesman pushing you toward a particular item, stop and think. What do your feelings tell you? If they tell you not to believe the salesman, then put your intuition to the test. Go ahead and buy the item you felt doubtful about. Take it home and use it. Within a short period of time you will find out if you were correct, or if that salesman really did know what he was talking about. One simple test like this should be enough to convince you that your intuitive impressions can be of great value.

I advise everyone I read for to begin paying more attention

to his or her own feelings and thoughts. Very often these sensations are trying to lead you in the right direction, to show you what some hidden section of your mind knows to be true. And still we pay no attention to these insights within us.

Who can estimate the help these intuitions could give us if we only bothered to listen to them? You might be able to avoid a bad business deal, prevent yourself from choosing the wrong marriage partner. Following your own thoughts might lead you to a new investment that will prove to be a gold mine. There is no one living today who could not benefit from paying more attention to his or her own psychic sixth sense. It is simply a matter of learning to trust yourself first before accepting everyone else's advice.

The Dream Diary

Dreams are another kind of psychic phenomenon that we all experience. No matter who you are, or what you do, your dreams carry important messages. Psychology tells us that many dreams are signals sent by our subconscious minds to dramatize problems or traumas we have not resolved. Such dreams are much like psychic visions in that they try to reveal a story that must be told. Such dreams are often disturbing, since they bring to mind something we are trying to forget or suppress.

Do not ignore these dreams! I recommend that you keep a pad and pencil near your bedside at all times. Should a dream wake you up in the middle of the night, take the time to write it down in as much detail as you can. Each morning when you awake, take a moment to put down in writing all the dreams you can remember. Again, be sure to be as specific and detailed as possible. You will soon find that some of your dreams are self-explanatory. For example, if you constantly dream that your husband is going out with another woman, you probably have a deep fear that he will do so and may be troubled by a fear that you will be abandoned. This emotion may be something that your conscious mind is not even aware of, and even if completely unfounded, it can cause you and your husband to drift apart. Should you find that your dreams involve painful emotions like these, it's best to discuss them with the other people involved—any woman who fears abandonment should take the time to tell her husband about her fears and doubts. Chances are, a little honest communication will eliminate her fears altogether.

Keeping notes of your dreams will also help you begin to see certain patterns. If a particular type of dream occurs over and over again, it is probably carrying a hidden message. Search your heart for the emotions that dream inspires. In these emotional responses you will find the meaning of the dream.

It is so unlikely that most people will ever experience the kind of dreams and visions I have that they need not worry about having them. But many people have more complex, uncommon dreams, some of which come very close to being the kind of psychic dreams I experience. Although these dreams may not be as powerful or precise, they do have precognitive qualities. For example, if you ever have a dream warning you of some danger, whether to yourself or to someone you love, do not take this lightly. Pay close, careful attention to dreams of warning, and take whatever steps possible to act on them. I do not know where such dreams come from. Nor do I claim to know where my own psychic visions originate. But they are far too clear and insistent to be ignored. And if you have dreams of warning, I suggest you too never ignore them.

Advice for the True Psychic

Every human being has some psychic power. If you believe you have more than others, you may want to heighten and develop you gift. Before you begin, it's important to be sure you *really* have such power. Here are a few indicators to look for:

—If you *consistently* find yourself knowing what someone will say before he speaks.

—If you *always* seem to know when the phone is about to ring, or when someone will soon arrive.

—If you ever think you can tell what someone else is thinking, especially if it contradicts completely what they are saying.

—If you *truly* feel you know what will happen next when there is no way to deduce it logically.

If any of these experiences occur regularly in your life, you may well be psychically gifted. If so, the first thing to do is to begin listening to your visions. These feelings, like the average person's intuition, are there to help you, and you will surely benefit if you follow what they recommend.

Just as you should keep a record of your dreams, also keep one of your visions. By writing them down as often as possible, you will be able to begin to study your powers and abilities. I know that during the years when I was struggling to understand and develop my gift, self-examination was of invaluable help. I tried to keep accurate records of all my visions, and I discovered that studying this list itself heightened my powers by building my confidence.

Another very good way to increase your ESP or precognitive powers is to study the field of parapsychology. Read as much scientific literature on the subject as you can find. Legitimate, respected scientists lately have written a lot about the world of psychic phenomena. Many of these books and reports can be found in your local library.

Another good source of information is the many books about the lives of famous psychics. I advise that you begin by reading about Edgar Cayce, probably the most gifted psychic of the modern age. His amazing accomplishments are well documented, and if Mr. Cayce's story does not convince you that psychic phenomena are real, then you weren't reading carefully enough! Reading about other psychics' lives was crucial for me during my formative years. It will help to get you into the proper frame of mind, essential to the prediction process. I no longer feel the need to study other psychics, but reading about them gave me strength when I was young and was filled with doubts.

I can't say enough about the importance of creating a positive mood and developing self-confidence. You must believe that other people can command this power, and believe that you are capable of it, too. For the same reason that it's good to surround yourself with information about the world of ESP, it's also wise to avoid exposing yourself to the doubts of nonbelievers. That is, if you constantly try to exercise your psychic powers when those around you are doubtful and scornful, you probably won't get anywhere.

Conducting Psychic Experiments—Think of a Number

The best policy is to find a friend who is also interested in this area, and try to exercise your psychic powers together. For example, if you have a friend who lives on the other side of town, the two of you can try a simple ESP experiment that should go something like this. At a prearranged time, each of you should be alone, at his or her own home, and in a relaxed and peaceful mood. During this time one of you should be the sender and the other the receiver.

The sender should spend about ten minutes concentrating as hard possible on a certain one- or two-digit number. In those ten minutes the receiver should try to keep his or her mind as clear and open as possible, avoiding extraneous thoughts. After the ten minutes have elapsed, call your partner and see what message he or she may have received. Be careful not to give any clues whatsoever. You may enjoy fooling yourself into believing that you have ESP but if you do this you really won't be accomplishing anything at all.

Be careful in evaluating the results of these experiments. If your partner fails to receive your message, this doesn't always mean you *don't* have ESP. Even those with the strongest powers can fail as often as they succeed. And in the same way, don't let a successful test go to your head. Many times success can be attributed to luck. The only way to get accurate results is to carry out tests like this one as many times as possible. You and your partner should try the message test for several weeks before trying to analyze the results conclusively. This way you can begin to eliminate the element of chance as a factor.

Picture Cards

Another useful ESP test involves picture cards. Each card shows a different shape—a circle, a star, an *X*, a square. One person selects a card, and concentrates on it, while the other—the subject—must try to use ESP to deduce which card has been selected. These cards can be made from a variety of household materials. On each card draw one of the shapes. Make several cards for each shape, and be sure the image you have drawn can not be seen from the reverse side.

When trying this experiment, again be sure to create a calm, relaxed atmosphere. Trying this test when you are tense, nervous, or excited will not provide accurate results. And again, keep nonbelievers out of sight. Do this experiment, or any other test of psychic powers, *only* with sincere, believing people. Just one nonbeliever in the room can completely destroy the psychic mood.

Just as with the message test, carry out the card test as many times as possible before trying to evaluate the results. Just as before, the higher the number of testings, the more you reduce the elements of chance and coincidence. If you discover that these tests are a success at least, ten percent of the time, say, then you can reasonably deduce that you may have psychic power that goes beyond common intuition. If so, continue your program of testing and development. First of all, if you haven't yet begun your intensive reading and study program, certainly begin right away. Read each and every book you can find on the subject of psychic phenomena. Take notes on anything in these volumes that is of interest to you, and write down any questions you may have about what you read.

Precognitive Playing Cards

Soon you should be ready for some new and more demanding tests, and can begin to discover what precognitive powers you have, if any.

Get a deck of common playing cards. With the help of your partner, try to predict which card will come up next in the deck. Unlike the message reading you did with the picture cards, this test has to do with trying to foresee an event in the *immediate* future.

This is far more difficult than the first two tests, and you should expect a lower percentage of successful predictions. If the odds earlier were ten to one and four to one, they are now fifty-two to one—so you can expect to be wrong a lot more often. But you can also take whatever success you have more seriously, too. With odds of fifty-two to one, the elements of chance and coincidence hardly come into play. After you repeat the test often enough, if you find that you are succeeding even as little as five percent of the time, then you can be certain that you have some degree of psychic ability.

Examining Your Motives

Once you have come this far successfully, it is time to do some hard soul-searching. There are a lot of questions you must ask yourself concerning your newly confirmed powers. First decide how far you want to go with the powers you have. For the most part, of course, the strength of your gift will make this decision for you, but there's a chance that you will soon develop extensive abilities. (The odds are very definitely against this happening, but the possibility exists.) So you must decide if you really want these powers to grow, or if you'd prefer to stop right where you are. Should you decide to go on to develop your powers, you will be entering an area of life few people ever experience. As you've seen in this book, psychic powers can bring as much sorrow as joy, as much pain as happiness. And this gift also brings with it many new responsibilities and obligations that you will not be able to sidestep.

To learn more about your own powers—how to strengthen them, how to understand them, how to use them wisely—I suggest you contact other psychics as soon as possible. In many cities there are psychic groups that hold seminars or classes in parapsychology—perfect places to share and to examine your experiences.

These other psychics, if legitimate, will be of great help, showing you how to exercise your power; they will be living examples of how to live with psychic abilities. And you will find that the company of psychics actually has a positive effect on your own powers.

As you continue your total program of psychic development, you will find that your gift is beginning to dominate your life. Being psychic is not like enjoying golf; it is not a hobby or pastime. It will take much of your energy and time—and if you ever reach the level I have, your gift may become a full-time occupation.

More Testing

The next step in experimentation is for you to try to make some personal predictions. Be certain to do so in complete confidentiality, however; do not tell your subject what you foresee. Although you may have abilities, you are not yet sure enough to begin shaping people's lives. Your visions will not be reliable yet for quite some time, so don't start warning people about things you see in their futures—you may be very, very wrong, and do more harm than good.

Try concentrating on a friend or loved one. Concentrate on his life, problems, interests, and see if you get any feelings about his future. If you do get some image, write it down immediately, but be certain not to speak of it to the subject. If you do mention it, you may not only be influencing them unfairly, you may also cause him to make your vision a reality. (It is not uncommon for clients to take a vision so seriously that they actually make it happen.) The power of suggestion can change your subject's future, so beware that you only predict events—not *cause* them.

And by keeping your vision to yourself, you can watch what happens to your subject and then see if your prediction was correct. But again, be careful not to fool yourself. Predicting that a pregnant friend will have a baby, or that a successful businessman will get a raise doesn't require psychic powers! Anyone, psychic or not, can predict the obvious. Try to wait for visions that are truly unique—*major* career changes, *new* love interests, *surprising* new successes or situations. If the vision is unusual or unexpected and does indeed come to pass, you can congratulate yourself on having made a successful prediction of the future.

The most important aspect of a successful test of this sort is that you prove you can make predictions *at will*. Your visions are not simply spontaneous. You are able to cause them simply by concentrating, thereby demonstrating some command over the gift you have. And once you've reached this point, you can begin to take some big steps forward.

From this point on, you should be in close contact with other psychics as much as possible. It may also be worthwhile to contact local colleges or institutes and inquire about their facilities for parapyschological research. If you find such facilities, volunteer as a research subject. I have been involved in such research several times as a subject, and have always found it a valuable experience that helps me attain a greater degree of self-confidence. And through the testing process you will learn a lot about your own powers.

But if you reach the later stages of psychic development, use caution, patience, and common sense. If you can, seek professional, scientific advice. Read as much as you can. Become acquainted with as many other psychics as you can. It is completely to your own advantage to test your powers rigorously before putting them to practical use. It is not an area to be rushed into. (I had been having psychic experiences for twenty years before I decided to become a professional.)

As you read this, I imagine you may be thinking that very little of it applies to you; and you may very well be right. But there is really no way of knowing unless you try the tests I have suggested—I have known several people who were virtually unaware of the strong psychic powers within them. This should not come as a surprise. Every one of us has some degree of psychic power, which only a very few are aware of. Instead of getting in touch with their powers of intuition and dreams, most people completely ignore their sixth sense. I often wonder how many have a great psychic potential that will never be developed.

You *can* develop psychic powers—by reading this book, you have already begun to create an attitude and atmosphere conducive to the growth and development of your gift. From this day on, make an effort to listen to those voices inside you. Pay attention to what they say, and do what they suggest. Learn to trust yourself and your feelings. You've got everything to gain—and nothing to lose.

15
Childhood, Death, and the Future

Many parents drag their children to me, insisting that the child is psychic. In the majority of cases the child is simply bright, and considers this whole business very strange indeed. These parents *want* their children to be psychic, just as some mothers want their sons to be doctors.

Is Your Child Psychic?

If you want to test your children's psychic ability, my advice is this: Let them be themselves. Don't try to force anything on them that doesn't come naturally. Then in time, if you notice that they actually do predict some events that they could not possibly have foreseen by normal means, give them a few little tests. Show them a picture of someone you know, but whom *they* have never met, and get their impressions of that person. They might very well come quite close to describing your friend. But if not, don't be discouraged—many times I am asked to make predictions for people, and absolutely nothing happens. Whatever you do, *don't give them any clues*. If you give them enough background information, most kids are bright enough to make accurate deductions. And if you test your child in this way, you will only be fooling yourself.

Remember: The child that you think is psychic may just be particularly bright or creative. So the chances that such a child could make accurate predictions are pretty high to begin with.

How to Raise Your Psychic Child

But suppose you actually do have a psychic child? How should you raise him or her?

My parents have often told me that despite the problems and tribulations, they were always glad to have me. Or at least that's what they say now! All things considered, my parents would be almost perfect models for parents of a psychically gifted child—except, perhaps, for the moments when they tried to deny what I was. I think there is a far better approach which would not leave the child as confused as I was.

Instead of discouraging the child, take the time to explain exactly what your fears are. A psychic child will almost always be very bright, and will understand exactly what you mean. Tell him or her that you understand this gift and believe in these powers. Never try to convince your child that he or she is imagining things that just happen to come true a few days later! Then explain that many people in this world do not believe in this gift, that some will consider him or her crazy, and that others who *do* believe may treat him or her like a freak or an alien. No child wants to be ostracized, and will quickly comprehend that you are trying to save him or her some pain.

Use the same methods that my parents did, and give such children all the freedom you can. Of course you should not tolerate bad behavior or cruelty. But when it comes to the children's interests and pursuits, let them have a free hand. Don't try to push them into anything but keep all the avenues of life open. If they like music, let them play piano or some other instrument. If they like sports, let them play baseball, football, or any game. Being a stage mother will only make a psychic child unhappy.

If you are truly convinced that your child is gifted, read books and articles about psychic phenomena. This is an area where I do *not* recommend that you follow my parents' path. When I was young they were unwilling to give me the facts, and I was starved for information about this confusing and frightening gift. Their unwillingness to inform me only made me want to know more. Although their intentions were good, they did not help by trying to keep me ignorant of the psychic world.

If your child is truly psychic, you will find it extremely difficult (perhaps impossible) to keep a secret. Your child may be quick to discover things you try to hide. This is especially true of a topic like sex, which most parents want to avoid until their kids reach a certain age. (I can remember being aware of sex *years* before anyone even hinted to me about it.) So, should your child express knowledge about this kind of thing, don't be upset. Psychic children can't help what they know. Don't accuse them of peeking into forbidden books, or eavesdropping on private conversations. If they are gifted, information simply comes to them. Many of these principles apply to raising *any* child, psychic or not. Certainly allowing your child intellectual freedom and not punishing inquisitiveness are good practices for all parents. Finally, if your child is psychic, I do not recommend that you push him or her toward being a professional.

This life is much like acting or entering the clergy—to be followed only if there is absolutely no way to live without doing so. If your child grows up to feel as I do, he or she will become a professional psychic without your encouragement. I myself had no interest in being a professional until I discovered that I simply had to. But it isn't bad, even though I would not recommend it to anyone—the emotions are simply too frightening and too *real* to be handled by anyone who is not very secure in his or her identity. Were I not fairly secure myself, I could not emerge still sane from some of my dreams.

Like any other child, a psychic child needs the security, acceptance, and understanding of a compassionate family. I thank God for giving me parents who gave me love when I needed comfort, corrected me when I was wrong, gave me strength when I felt weak and afraid—and to this day, give unquestioning, unqualified love.

I hope my gift enables people to understand the future and

the role they play in shaping it. Whenever possible, I try to show people how they can change their own lives in the days ahead. And when the forces of fate are in control, I want to help people avoid any disasters they possibly can. All in all, I have been happy with the clients I've served and with the advice I've given. I am almost always able to help people deal with whatever is troubling them, and I'm glad that personal advice—unlike predictions of disasters and plane crashes—is one area where I can see my visions put to use. The wonderful feeling of seeing someone benefit from my help makes everything worthwhile.

Hard as it may be to believe, the most saddening aspect is that the whole process cannot continue forever. I know I will someday die, as we all must—I have even foreseen the circumstances of my death. I do believe in an afterlife, although I can't attempt to describe things beyond this world. But like most people, I would like to live forever.

Psychics and Death

I am confronted with death—or at least the vision of it—almost every day, so I have found it necessary to form a straightforward, commonsense approach. I do not enjoy the idea of death, but I certainly realize it is unavoidable. And I do not think that we human beings should delude ourselves into believing that the finality of death can be so easily overcome—or that the dead can return, or even make contact with us.

I also have formed some opinions concerning the principles that should guide the use of psychic powers. There are psychic practices and activities that I strongly disapprove of, both for moral and for scientific reasons. For example, I am opposed to the whole area of contact with the dead. First, I believe it is morally wrong; second, I don't believe it really happens.

I try to approach death calmly and logically. Trying to find proof that ghosts exist or struggling to make contact with the dead seems foolish.

Even though I do believe in an afterlife, to me, death is undeniably final. I do not think there can be any coming back over the brink. And if the dead did want to make contact with the living, why would they need me? Certainly they would be capable of communicating on their own, without the help of a psychic or medium. In my opinion, we must assume that the dead simply do not wish to talk to us—or they would have done so a long time ago! Let's leave the dead to rest in peace. God knows I wouldn't want anyone calling me back—if I've got something to say to someone, I'll say it myself!

I also believe that all the self-proclaimed psychics who claim to be able to put clients in contact with loved ones and friends who have passed away are phonies and rip-off artists. My advice would be not to waste your money on them.

I am also not convinced of reincarnation—the experiments claiming that an adult can be hypnotized and then begin to speak a foreign language do not, in my opinion, provide conclusive proof—there are too many other possible explanations. Perhaps the person is picking up this new language psychically, or maybe just has an extraordinary imagination. Or maybe the experiment is just not legitimate. Seeing a *child* speak Latin under hypnosis might convince me to believe in reincarnation. In the meantime I will continue to consider it just another delusion that clouds the real issue of psychic powers.

The problem, really, is not simply that the issue needs to be resolved, but that first it has to be defined. Ther are currently so many false psychics around the world, and so many unrelated subjects that are lumped into the same psychic phenomena category, that the important questions have not yet been isolated from all the rhetoric surrounding the issue.

But the situation is beginning to improve. The Stanford Research Institute, the Parapsychology Foundation, and other respected scientific organizations have begun intensive and thorough investigations into the nature and function of psychic phenomena. I truly hope that their work will result in a new understanding of psychics like myself, and if the work of these organizations comes to be respected as scientifically valid, it will lend additional respectability to all legitimate psychics.

This kind of research can yield fascinating and conclusive

results. I have myself attempted several research studies. Over several years' time, for example, I tried to determine whether there is some relationship between plane crashes and certain dates or months in the year. I discovered that plane crashes *do* tend to happen on particular days of the month, and can almost be predicted on this basis.

It seems that the cycles of the moon have a distinct effect. Plane crashes are more likely to take place when a new phase of the moon begins—full moon, new moon, first or last crescent. It seems to me that this information could help psychics; it also points to the usefulness of consulting astrological patterns in making predictions. I believe strongly in astrology, so it doesn't surprise me that the moon can so easily influence events on earth.

With a little luck and lots of hard work, there will soon be enough scientific evidence to make people start paying greater attention to legitimate psychics, and perhaps prevent some of the tragedies so often predicted but never avoided.

Changing the Future

The key question about psychic phenomena concerns the actual nature of what we call the future. Is it fixed, controlled by destiny, impossible to change? Or does it change constantly as human beings make decisions and choices? Do our actions shape the future, or is it shaped by the outside hand of fate? I have spent countless hours considering this very complex and confusing question. It seems to me that future events can be broken down into two categories: Events we cause, and events that cause themselves.

There are many aspects of your future that you directly control. If you do a bad job at work, for example, you may be fired. If you work hard, you may be promoted. And if you were to ask me about the security of your career, what I could tell you would be nothing more accurate than this.

The exceptions come when the actions of others affect you directly. Then your future is shaped by the wills and actions of more than just yourself. And this is the way it is for most of us. There are very few things in life that we alone can control. Someone else is almost always involved. So a large part of what is to come is a little like a football game. Fate does not decide the winner; the combined actions of the players determine the outcome.

For the most part, the future is not fixed or determined. Rather, it changes from day to day as people decide to do one thing and not another. And this is why the predictions I make for people often change from one session to the next. Over a week's time I can receive two completely different impressions of a person's future. It's certainly possible that in some cases this reversal is caused by my own mistakes. But I think the true explanation is that the clients themselves—or someone else in the situation—have taken some action that has altered the future. Because my clients believe deeply in my gift, it is not unusual for them to take action right away on the basis of my predictions. These actions can result in drastic changes for the future, so when they consult with me again, their futures may have changed completely.

But other aspects of the future do indeed seem fixed and determined. Natural disasters like earthquakes are certainly not influenced by what you or I do in our personal lives. These fixed events are part of the natural processes of the universe. Floods, earthquakes, some fires, and other disasters come under this heading. Still other events simply seem to be predestined by fate, or perhaps by the will of God. Most of us will die not in freak accidents, but rather at a very definite and prearranged time. For the most part, I believe there is little we can do about these facts of life. Sometimes I have dream-visions of terrible tragedies that are so powerful, so definite, that I sense they could not be prevented even if the proper authorities were to heed my warnings.

And somewhere between these two extremes lies the secret that can explain all of life. For everything that happens is either an act of God or an act of man—half our experiences are beyond our control, while the other half are the direct result of who and what we are.

For now, the psychic must struggle with the confusion and uncertainty of limited understanding. Much like the science of medicine, which was practiced for centuries before any major breakthroughs occurred, parapsychology will probably have to limp along for many years before our understanding greatly expands.

There will be a breakthrough someday, though. Science will discover the source of psychic visions, and man will begin to understand the true nature of these phenomena. Once this happens, psychic powers will finally be used to benefit mankind, to improve the way we live—and to change the future forever. In the meantime, psychics like me will remain modern Cassandras—able to foresee tragedy, only to be ignored. I will continue to see newspaper stories about other psychics making amazingly accurate predictions being published only after the predicted tragedy has already taken place. Meanwhile, stop for a moment and join me in a very special prayer:

> With the infinite good that is within me, I pray to the infinite good that is within you, dear God. And with the infinite good that is within you, dear God, please pray for the infinite good that is within me.

16
Predictions for a New Decade

Imagine what you will be doing five or ten years from today. What will our lives be like? How many alarming, even amazing changes will come to pass? How many wonderful discoveries and inventions will improve the way we live, day in and day out? And what terrible disasters, world crises, and wars will bring sorrow and death to our fellow human beings?

Five years ago, could you have foreseen the hostage crisis in Iran? The People's Temple tragedy? The election of Pope John Paul II? The Mount St. Helens volcano eruption?

In all time, in each and every decade of human history, there are shocking developments, astounding new achievements, and unexpected calamities. In my life I have experienced a strange phenomenon: I can foresee a great number of the details and intricacies of our future. Every week, in dreams or disturbing visions, I experience what has not yet occurred, living through events that are yet to come. Some are the fine details of clients' destinies, while others are visions of major events that will rock society on this earth, and influence every life.

When these predictions occur, I may be shaken and disturbed by their power and brilliance, but I make certain to note them in my diary. From time to time I review them and compare the various predictions. Sometimes I discover that two visions are actually part of one prediction, like separate pieces of the same puzzle. Alone, each is confusing, meaningless.... But when combined, their secret is revealed. Like when lamp and bulb are brought together, there is light.

In recent months I have made many predictions concerning our future. Some concern politics, wars, and international events. Others describe earthquakes, storms, and disasters. Still more are visions of scientific breakthroughs—some of which will benefit man, and some that can only destroy him.

As we've discussed before, there is always a personal aspect to my predictions. When I experience a vision of the future, I comprehend it in light of my own feelings and interests. I consider what the vision will mean to *my* society—the American people. Whether it be a world crisis or an earthquake, the meaning of each vision is filtered through my mind, and my perspective reflects my alliances.

For this reason, the following predictions are of particular importance to you. For the most part they describe future events that will directly influence your family, neighbors, and friends. If my percentage of accuracy remains constant, the vast majority of these events will indeed come to pass within the near future—perhaps this very year. Mark these predictions and remember them—they will change the fabric of your life and can be of service to you. Reflect on them, come back and reread them again later on. The messages are clear and vitally important.

There are fifty-nine predictions listed here, but by the time you read this book, I will have fifty-nine more. Time does not pause: Present turns to past, and future becomes today. And with each moment, the future stretches further out in front of us, and there are new events to foresee.

1. On a recent primary day, when my mind was filled with thoughts of our political future, I found myself awakened in the middle of the night. My television set was on, and the volume was turned up to its maximum. I must have fallen asleep watching TV, I recall thinking. Then a vision came. I saw people with two-way television sets—regular TVs with special cable boxes attached, allowing the viewer to respond to what was said on the program. In

the vision, I saw a typical couple watching the two-way TV set. But they were not watching for pleasure; they were actually voting for political candidates. Then I heard an announcer on this wondrous new television set explaining that this was a presidential primary election. People were voting for President by television! I predict, then, that within the next few years—perhaps in our very next presidential election—vast numbers of Americans will be voting via two-way TV!

2. While strolling along a Long Island beach, I had a vision that concerned light—bright light emerging from darkness. The light grew pure white, almost blinding. Then, when the light softened, I could see a surgical procedure being performed. Doctors, using many technical devices, were implanting a lens in a woman's eye. The lens would replace the woman's eyeglasses. She would never wear glasses again, and the new lens would remain implanted permanently. I even sensed that this lens might be adjustable, should the woman's optical needs change in any way in the future. Thus the lens could be altered without removal. In the future, then, I predict that almost no one will wear eyeglasses or contact lenses, but rather will use amazing new lenses implanted permanently in the human eye.

3. Here's a prediction that was frightening for me. While giving a personal consultation to a New York scientist, whom I won't name, I was suddenly overcome by a powerful vision. I saw several men bundled in heavy clothes to protect them from the freezing winds atop a snow-capped mountain peak. The men were wielding large, heavily woven nets against the driving gales, apparently attempting to capture some great and powerful beast. And then I saw the creature. Shaped like a giant of a man, but larger still and far stronger, it seemed to stand more than eight feet tall and was covered with fur, as though it were wrapped in a heavy pelt. It was the yeti, or big foot, as it is sometimes called. In the near future, a yeti will be captured—alive and well—on the treacherous slopes of the Himalayas.

4. Sadly, many of my recent visions of tomorrow show growing hunger and starvation in some parts of the world. In one dream I saw little African children dying slowing of malnutrition, starvation, and disease. At the same time, their parents and elders were driven to battle with neighboring societies for what little food could be had. When this food was gone, the people resorted to cannibalism for survival. It sounds too horrifying to be possible, but cannibalism will soon become a common practice in some parts of Africa.

5. Another prediction revealed that in the years to come—hopefully, quite soon—a little-known scientist, working with virtually no economic support in a back-country section of South America, will discover an amazing medical process. He will isolate a serum which, with just one injection, will immunize people from *all tropical diseases for life!* Word of his breakthrough will spread quickly, and while the medical establishment will be slow to recognize his genius, the unknown lifesaver's vaccine will soon be given to people all over the world, eliminating many dangerous diseases from the earth.

6. For those who suffer with them, bunions and other foot problems are agony. Now there is hope for these people. In a vision I could see that in the next few years a fabulous development will come to pass. People will be able to use a wonderful at-home surgery kit to remove painful bunions once and for all. The kit will be easy to use, completely safe, and thoroughly effective in almost all cases. And in addition, it won't cost much money!

7. For those interested in coin collecting, finance, or international currency, there will soon be a surprising change. Two major European nations (probably France, England, or Germany) will change the coins they use as currency within a single year. The new coinage will be actively sought by collectors, and will have a strong positive effect on the economy of Europe and the Western world. Also, the new coins will make the old currency more valuable. So if

you are holding onto a collection of European coins, it might be wise to keep them a few years more.

8. The rain and runoff problems in California are going to get worse with each passing year, leading finally to a terrible flood in the San Fernando Valley. A long and powerful rainstorm will produce massive floods. Before the damage is over, many people will die, including at least one famous celebrity. Millions of dollars of destruction will occur to property and crops. The site will be declared a disaster area, and the government will spend millions of dollars searching for a solution to this annual problem.

9. In another dream prediction that left me in a terrible state of shock for several hours, I was able to foresee increasing earthquake activity in California. One extremely powerful earthquake will occur soon, more destructive and devastating than any in the recent past. In my dream, I saw a large skyscraper—one of the few in L.A.—rocking back and forth. All of Los Angeles will be shaken by this quake, and some people will die. That skyscraper will come within a hairbreadth of toppling to the ground below. Many of the people inside will be injured, but none of them will die.

10. I had another waking vision of medical progress. Again, I saw someone undergoing an operation, this time in a medical clinic in the southwestern United States. Scientists specializing in neurosurgery will discover a link between a tiny nerve in the spine and the loss of mobility. They will then develop a surgical technique to manipulate this spinal nerve, and thus restore the ability to walk to people who have been crippled since birth. The technology will take some time to spread, but eventually millions of crippled people will benefit from this joyful discovery.

11. Still another scientific prediction came to me recently. As it happens, I was strolling on a spring day through the Central Park Zoo in New York City. As I stood before the monkey cages, a vision of scientific study came to mind. I saw two scientists

somewhere right here in New York experimenting with laboratory animals. The scientists had successfully transplanted the brains of two monkeys into each other. Both monkeys survived and were in good condition. In time, this breakthrough will lead to tremendous medical miracles for mankind, and also to some dangerous plots and conspiracies by powerful people who dream of eternal life. All this will happen before the year 1990.

12. Experts studying the life of sea animals will also make a surprising breakthrough. The secret language of the dolphins will be deciphered. After years of recording "conversations" between these creatures, researchers will be able to break their code and actually find ways to talk with dolphins. This will lead to conclusive proof that the dolphin is as intelligent as man; the future possibilities from this breakthrough are limitless. Again, this discovery will be used for both good and evil purposes.

13. A few weeks ago I was walking along the East River when a frightening yet awe-inspiring vision came to me. I was looking south, toward the United Nations building, when suddenly I dreamed I saw a giant spaceship hovering over the building. A smaller ship, something of a dinghy for the mother ship, descended to earth, where a group of international ambassadors awaited its landing. In a way, this vision frightened me, but it also made me happy—joyous that contact with our fellow residents of this universe had been accomplished. I predict, therefore, that within the next few years, conclusive proof of the existence of UFOs will be presented to the world through the United Nations. The proof will be so undeniable, and there will be so many witnesses in so many countries, that no intelligent person will ever doubt the presence of UFOs again.

14. Our continuing experimentations with germ warfare—often top secret and kept hidden from the public—will eventually lead to disaster. A strange new form of bacteria, developed in the laboratory, will accidentally be unleashed on the America public. The bacteria will escape when the train it is transported on derails

somewhere in the South. The killer bacteria will spread quickly across the country (as it is designed to do), and an epidemic will result. Some of our nation's enemies will consider using this disaster as an opportunity to invade and conquer us, but an amazing act of nature will negate the effects of the bacteria, and we will be safe. Only a small number of people will actually be harmed, but for several weeks terror will reign across vast sections of America.

15. In either the next presidential election or the one to follow, a candidate representing a new political party will run and receive a very large percentage of the vote. This party will find support among both conservatives and liberals, and its main platform will be to cut taxes and improve the economy, which may be in very disastrous condition by that time. The candidate has a good chance of winning, as his base of support is very strong. Win or lose, this candidate will split the vote for *both* of the other candidates, and thus will determine the outcome of the election.

16. A few weeks ago, I was shocked from my sleep by a dream of death and killing. I saw soldiers fighting in a warm climate, and many civilians—women and children as well as young men—lay dead in the streets. I predict that within the near future, Israel and Lebanon will go to war. Iran and the PLO will play a vital role, and Egypt will make history by supporting the Israelis. The outcome of the war is uncertain, but both the U.S. and Russia will be actively involved. If it lasts long enough, this struggle could lead to World War III.

17. I've got good news and bad news for TV watchers. (That includes just about all of us, I presume.) After a long battle, cable television will overtake commercial television as America's most popular form of entertainment. For a few short months, cable TV will be wonderful. But then the cable companies will give in to the tremendous potential profits, and some commercials will be included on the air. This will still be an improvement, however, since it will give every American, no matter where he lives, a choice from dozens of television channels.

18. Lately I had a dream of traveling through the skies at a speed faster than any plane has ever traveled. It was a fighter plane designed by one of the giant defense companies, and it will travel faster than the supersonic Concorde. The plane will give tremendous superiority to American military forces, and may help avoid war. In time, the technology used to produce such amazing speed will be applied to passenger flights as well.

19. In another dream I found myself relaxing in comfort on the largest flying machine ever built. This plane was far larger than a 747, holding more than 600 passengers! The plane will be in full operation by 1990, and it will run so efficiently that air fares then may actually be lower than they are now!

20. The growing problem of mass transit, coupled with a shortage of energy, will lead to several new forms of public transportation before the end of the eighties. Among these new ways of getting around will be a sophisticated system of monorails and elevated train lines. The new trains will move faster than any subways currently in existence, will be far less noisy, and a lot more comfortable. Either New York or Chicago will be the first city to build this system, but it will eventually be in use in cities around the world. The monorails will also use less energy and create less pollution than conventional trains.

21. This next prediction was quite eerie and disturbing. I believe this is something that will come to pass far into the future, perhaps several decades into the next century, because all the people and the buildings in this vision were unlike any on earth. The people seemed taller than most of us, and they wore strange clothes made from fabric I could not recognize. The buildings were odd shaped and large, made entirely of a golden glass. The development revealed to me in this dream is a pill, an apparently simple medicine that amazingly can increase the IQ of anyone who takes it. I predict that in the next century everyone will take this pill, and each of them will have an IQ above the genius level, even greater than Albert Einstein's!

22. As time moves on, people will begin to form towns and communities in parts of the planet we once thought uninhabitable. From the poles to the deserts, new communities will blossom, made of new and revolutionary buildings. These buildings will be completely constructed of modules—sections—stacked on top of each other, or laid side by side. These modules will be movable, and it will not be uncommon for a whole city to be transported. In addition, some of the buildings will actually be adjustable, able to grow larger or smaller, depending on need.

23. The current progress in the field of electronics—already moving forward in leaps and bounds—will increase. The next few years will see a new electronic revolution, with new discoveries as earthshaking as the telephone or the light bulb. A new kind of computer, capable of human thought and communication, will be developed in the U.S., aiding the cure of diseases, the further development of technology, and even more electronic discoveries. The devices will begin to create and improve themselves!

24. While reading the financial news on a day not long ago, I suddenly found myself reading an article that was not actually in the paper. Before my eyes I saw a news story not yet written. It told of an amazing new alloy, made from some of the most common and abundant metals on earth, that will replace silver in industrial use and as jewelry. A panic will result in the silver market, sending prices down at a disastrous pace. But in time, real silver for jewelry will become prized and rare as gold—and nearly as expensive!

25. Another prediction related to jewelry: A small businessman in the industry will accidentally develop a powerful new glue made from completely natural ingredients. The news of this discovery will shock the jewelry business, but more importantly, it will also be noticed by the medical establishment. Heart specialists will prove that this organic glue can actually be used to mend damaged arteries around the heart. In the years to come, many people undergoing bypass surgery will actually be having their arteries glued together, with amazing success and minimal risk.

26. Within the next ten years, the field of dentistry will be revolutionized. Preventive dentistry is already a growing area of medical procedure, but soon a young dentist will create an amazing once-a-year toothpaste, or coating, which, when applied by a dentist, will virtually prevent all cavities from forming. While we will all still brush our teeth daily, this annual treatment will insure the continued health of our teeth. Imagine never getting another cavity as long as you live! Picture every child in America with a beautiful, flawless smile. Within a few years, it will be so!

27. For the heavy drinkers out there, get ready for a new and powerful potable to tempt your tastebuds. This new drink, made of a totally new kind of chemical agent similar to alcohol, will have the equivalent potency of a two-hundred-proof whiskey. The new booze will be sold under several brand names, but the "two-hundred-proof" claim will be part of the marketing. The new liquor should be available in a few years, but look out! One sip of this stuff and it's "bon voyage!"

28. The years ahead will bring cures for many of the diseases that now plague us, as well as methods of correcting physical problems we always thought incurable. Believe it or not, a drug will be isolated that can actually cause missing limbs and organs to grow back. This regeneration process will be tricky and delicate, but many people who now have missing limbs may find themselves growing new ones by the 1990s. I had this prediction in a dream, in which I saw a man with one regular arm and a second that was actually growing in. The vision was unpleasant, like looking at a circus freak. But the benefits of this drug will be astounding for many crippled people.

29. The reign of terror that now plagues our world will not disappear in the near future. Terrorists and other revolutionaries will develop new and devilish methods for wreaking havoc and destruction. Among these techniques will be the use of pigeons and other birds in guerrilla warfare. The birds will be trained to carry small explosives to intended targets, killing people without warning, and giving the benefit of surprise to the revolutionaries. Many

other evil tricks will also be employed by senseless terrorists and anarchists in the next few years, as world strife continues undiminished.

30. As world conflicts increase and cold war methods grow between us and the Russians, all kinds of espionage will be used. Trained psychics will be brought into government service with the purpose of psychically "eavesdropping" on foreign embassies and consulates. These psychics will provide government agents with top-secret inside information about the actions of foreign agents in the world. I have had a dream in which I myself am involved in an espionage attempt.

31. Indira Gandhi, now restored to power, will continue to fight back against dissidents and revolutionaries in her land. But soon the problems of India and accusations of corruption in her government will lead to her overthrow by a revolutionary group, or a coalition of several groups who oppose her. She will probably flee India, and the friendliness of the new government toward the United States will be doubtful at best.

32. Surprisingly, the eastern United States will also have its share of earthquakes in the days and years ahead. One large earthquake, centered in New Hampshire, will do a large amount of damage. The tremors will be felt from Boston to Buffalo, and many cities in the East will be damaged to some degree. At Niagara Falls, power generators and cables will be destroyed, causing another major blackout in New York State and other surrounding areas. The earthquake will result in a few deaths. It will also unearth artifacts from ancient cultures which will be discovered many years later by a farm boy.

33. Although many people thought the battle against pollution was being won, our present concerns about energy are leading us back to our polluting ways. Before the present energy crisis is solved, the level of pollution in our air and water will reach a new

high, exceeding the degree it reached just a few years ago. This pollution will result in many new health problems for all Americans, including heightened risk of health and lung diseases, as well as cancer. This dangerous pollution level will lead to an even greater public outcry for efficient, abundant new energy sources.

34. Another terrifying dream I had recently concerned that charming and charismatic man, Pope John Paul II. He is on another world tour in this vision, speaking to a giant throng in Asia. During his sermon a man in the crowd, suffering from mental disorders, leaps up and begins firing a pistol at the pope. Fortunately, the pope will escape harm, although others in the crowd will be injured. This event will not deter the pope from his travels.

35. In still another vision, I dreamed I was talking to a woman who must have been one hundred years old or more. She was completely lucid and lively, talking and chatting like a girl of sixteen. She explained to me that an amazing nutritional program had been developed to prevent senility, and to cure it in those who had suffered with it for years. This woman told me that by the year 2000 no one would ever grow senile again. People would remain alert and functional well into their nineties or beyond; and coupled with other breakthroughs, people could be living and working to the age of one hundred or even years after that centennial birthday party!

36. A few days later I had a second vision in which I spoke with the same woman. This time she told me of an amazing new fountain-of-youth drug she was taking. The pill was a safe combination of natural ingredients that extended people's life span by as much as 50 percent. Her doctor had said she could expect to live to be 150 years old! She told me the drug was discovered in the late 1980s and put into full use a few months later. She also told me not to worry about dying, and to save up lots of money for retirement, because I may be living to the age of 200!

37. The science of oceanography is about to experience some brilliant new breakthroughs leading to the discovery of vast riches beneath the earth's seas. Very soon, technology will be developed to allow explorers to remain below the ocean's surface for more than one full year. This will allow scientists to form testing labs and even research stations deep below the sea. In a very short period of time this new development will lead to the mining of the ocean's bottom, where tons of valuable minerals—as well as precious oil—will be uncovered and reclaimed for human use.

38. Jerry Brown is right: The space program will be reborn, and it will play a vital role in our future. We will begin to explore our solar system, establishing bases and outposts on many of our neighboring planets. At one such base on the planet Uranus, a new mineral will be discovered. It will be much like diamond, but with unique properties not found in the hardest of our metals. This amazing new stone will have the ability to bend and refract light as no man-made lens can, and it will lead to a new revolution in laser technology.

39. In the early stages of this new exploration of space, astronomers will discover a planet which had been unnoticed in our solar system. The planet will fascinate scientists and science-fiction writers for many years, well into the next century. This new planet will also fascinate astrologers, and it will be used to explain many of the amazing powers of the zodiac. After this new planet is found, astrology will at last become a fully accepted science around the globe.

40. By the late 1990s we will have established a military base on the moon. Many astronauts and scientists will live and work there year round. I recently experienced a vision of this base. With the earth glowing strangely in the sky above, men worked; children went to school; and people lived full, normal lives on the moon's harsh surface. An asteroid, much like those that formed the craters on the moon, will plummet through space and strike our moon base, doing extensive damage and leaving many of the set-

tlers stranded. A major rescue mission will be undertaken as a cooperative effort of several nations, and the moon dwellers will be saved.

41. As we near the year 2000, history will repeat itself. From the Middle East, perhaps the Sinai, a man will emerge whom people will follow with faith and devotion. The man will be called a healer by some and a prophet by others. Within a few years this man will have a following all around the world, and some will be calling him the second Christ. My vision of this man is not yet completely formed, and I cannot say if his effect will be for good or evil. But he will arrive, and his presence will be known to all the world.

42. In another vision I could see two politicians waving triumphantly to a jubilant crowd. The two men clasped hands in the air in a combined victory gesture, to the wild cheers of their supporters. What I saw was a victory party to be celebrated after a presidential election in the near future. Essentially, this election and victory party will be like most others: lots of promises, speeches, and sloganeering. But this time there will be one unique distinction. It will herald the arrival of America's first black Vice-President. This all will happen within the next three presidential terms.

43. In France, the Eiffel Tower will be damaged by fire. The fire will occur in summer, at the height of the tourist season, and on a particularly active day—a Saturday, I believe. Several tourists will be injured in this disaster. The fire will be caused by an electrical problem in the lights that illuminate the structure by night. Fortunately, the number of deaths and injuries, as well as the damage to the tower, will be kept to a minimum by effective, dedicated, and efficient firemen.

44. Women's fashions go through some strange periods now and then, and in the next few years we will be seeing the strangest trend in a long, long time. Believe it or not, Roman togas

will be in fashion. Cut just like in movies such as *Cleopatra,* the togas will show lots of shoulder and bosom. Women will wear them both for work and socializing, with more- or less-glamorous materials used in the different gowns. Some enterprising women will discover that these new fashions can be made at home from purchased materials within a few short minutes of work. Cut, snip, stitch, and you've got a high-fashion toga! This trend to make your own clothes will cause the fashion industry to dump the toga idea within one short season. Thank goodness!

45. The world of police work and crime prevention will be aided by continued improvement in lie-detector machines, and a new device will also make it easier to determine guilt or innocence. This amazing device, which should be discovered in about eight years, will actually be able to scan the electronic signals that pass through our minds and read the thoughts of whomever is being analyzed. The device will be considered for a wide variety of uses, from spying on competitive industries to sizing up the feelings of lovers. But government regulation will keep these devices off the open market well into half of the next century.

46. Last week I had another of those terrifying dreams of the future that sometimes make me wish I were not psychic. I saw what at first looked like a vision of Jim Jones's day of death in Guyana. A religious leader of some sort was prompting a large group of followers to their death. Many people already lay dead on the ground. But as the terrifying dream continued on its gruesome path, I saw that this was not the People's Temple, but rather a *new* cult in California. I believe this event will come to pass before the 1980's are over. I am not sure how many people will die in this cult tragedy, but it will be as senseless and terrible an event as the People's Temple disaster.

47. While the world outcry against nuclear weapons will continue, and although most world governments will attempt to curb the arms race and protect the world, a nuclear tragedy will occur. A military bomber, armed with a nuclear warhead, will accidentally deploy a missile while cruising over Australia. I cannot

say how much damage this weapon will do; my vision only shows it being launched. I also do not know whether an American or Soviet plane will be involved. The potential destruction is quite extensive, so I have decided to warn our government about this vision. I hope the event can be avoided, for all our sakes.

48. About one month ago I had a vision that was very strong and clear, and yet also rather confusing. I saw a pregnant woman in a doctor's office. The doctor was giving her a bottle filled with small pills. I still do not know exactly how, but this little pill would determine the sex of her unborn child. That is, she could choose whether she wanted a son or a daughter, and take the appropriate pill. I am afraid I cannot explain the medical processes involved, but somehow, soon, a pill will be produced that will let you choose the sex of your children.

49. Another major area of change in our collective future will concern what we eat. More and more people will turn from the foods that are now killing us to foods that can help our bodies stay healthy and young. For one thing, Americans will consume almost no beef at all in the future. The beef industry will virtually cease to exist. Other more wholesome foods will replace beef, and in a short time a whole new form of cuisine will become popular, using these new beef substitutes. In time they will be considered standard food fare, and not a replacement at all. If you are thinking of investing in cattle, watch your step!

50. On the international scene, the government of Turkey will be overthrown, perhaps within the next few months. This will present the Russians with an excellent opportunity to expand their sphere of influence, and in fact, they might induce the revolution in Turkey. Either way, this NATO country will become a hotbed of international dispute within the very near future. The President may call for drastic action to contain the Russians and to oppose Communist forces who may desire control of Turkey. Whether this comes to pass in the next months, or as long as a few years from now, make no mistake: The present government of Turkey cannot last.

51. In another medical discovery, surgeons will begin to use an advanced form of magnetism to help the healing process in broken bones. This concept will be the brainstorm of a few unknown physical therapists in the United States. The magnetism will be used to hold the bones tightly together, inducing a faster knit and quicker healing. This discovery should occur before 1986.

52. After years of effort, after countless hours of appealing to our charitable natures, Jerry Lewis will see his life's dream come true. The money he has raised in the last decades from his annual telethon for muscular dystrophy will finally produce a cure. Thousands of children around the world will benefit from this breakthrough, and Jerry will be honored by the governments of many countries around the world. The annual contributions he received will continue to increase each year until this time. Once the cure is found, tax money will be used to supply it to those who are suffering from muscular dystrophy. This should occur within ten or twelve years.

53. The Golden Gate Bridge will be badly damaged by an earthquake. This will result in the closing of the bridge for many months as extensive repairs will have to be made. Ferry service will be formed to facilitate travel below the closed bridge. I am not certain, but believe this destruction will occur in the same series of earthquakes that will rock all of California.

54. On the other side of the world, earthquakes will damage the oldest landmark of the Chinese, who will undertake the full rebuilding of the Great Wall. A five-year program will be formed specifically for this purpose. American technology may even be used to facilitate the repairs to the Great Wall, further solidifying our new bonds with the Chinese people.

55. Major changes can also be seen in the climate and weather of our planet. Within the next two decades, a shifting of the earth's axis will take place, as it did thousands of years ago. This shift will result in warmer temperatures at the poles, causing the melting of large sections of frozen earth and glacial structures.

This water will spill into the seas, evaporate into the atmosphere, and eventually find its way to land, where massive floods will result. Meteorologists are already predicting such changes in the earth's climate. I can tell you with certainty that they will indeed occur.

56. Natural forces similar to those which will cause this melting and the earthquakes will also cause a tidal wave in the Pacific. I cannot give an exact year, but many of these violent thrusts and upheavals within the earth's core may come back to back, in rapid succession. The tidal wave will do a great deal of damage to South Pacific islands, and the Hawaiian island of Maui will be largely destroyed. Many people will die in this disaster, and many others left homeless. Those remaining will be moved to other islands or brought back to the coastal U.S. As a result of this tidal wave, the popularity of Hawaii as a vacation spot will be greatly decreased.

57. Perhaps in the same series of natural forces and stresses, Mt. Etna in Italy will erupt, causing the loss of thousands of lives. It will spit fire and spew molten rock for many weeks, and a large portion of the local population will be evacuated. This prediction came to me in a dream filled with flashing flames, thunderous explosions, and the screams of villagers fleeing the all-destroying lava. This eruption will come largely as a surprise to the experts (as has Mount St. Helens), who will believe Etna to be quiet and sleeping up until the final days before it explodes. The damage, destruction, deaths, and injuries resulting from the Mt. Etna explosions will be very, very extensive.

58. In another recent dream I stood inside the control room of a nuclear power plant in northern California. The scene I witnessed was almost an exact duplicate of a segment from the film *China Syndrome.* The technicians manning the control room went into a panic; loud noises could be heard rumbling deep within the facility; and lights and alarms flashed on the electronic devices that filled the laboratory-like room. The vision ended before I could discover how much damage might be done, and in recent days I

have been hoping a second dream would occur to more fully explain this tragedy. Right now I cannot describe the exact amount of damage. But I can predict one thing with certainty: A meltdown very definitely will occur at a large nuclear plant in northern California. It might be that each of these last few disasters and changes in our environment will all be caused by the same series of shifts and eruptions within the earth.

59. The last prediction I will share with you is good news indeed. Very shortly, a large deposit of oil will be discovered in Nebraska and South Dakota. This oil will be high quality, and also very easy to drill for. Once this oil is found, our nation will immediately cut down its dependence on the OPEC nations. The discovery will also dramatically strengthen the standing of the dollar overseas, thus booming our economy, and also helping us ease over the rest of the present energy crisis until new energy sources are developed and put into practical use. (One bonus prediction: The energy crisis will be solved. We will find an alternative source of power. Our nation will survive this current threat, just as it has survived so many others in the past.)

Every day, such elements of our future occur. Some of them are foreseen by people like myself, others go unpredicted until they actually take place. The above 59 events lie in wait for us in the years to come. If you are in the first quarter of your life, you will probably see each of these events occur before you die (especially if we all really do wind up living to 150!).

As time moves on, keep your eyes open for the events I have described. Sometimes the minor details may be a little different. Perhaps it will be an injection, not a pill, that will give you power over the sex of unborn child. The important point is that the breakthroughs will occur; the progress will be made. And if my words are heeded, hopefully the tragedies can be minimized.

17

The Psychic Revolution—and Fulfilling Your Personal Destiny

Without question, the past decade has seen a tremendous change in society's attitudes toward psychic phenomena. When I was a child, only a few people even knew what that expression referred to. Everyone had heard of séances, ghosts, and mediums, but no one put any faith in them or considered them to be anything more than a lot of hocus-pocus.

And then suddenly, all at once, the world was dying to know what would happen to their favorite stars during the months to come. People like me were appearing on magazine covers. We became media personalities.

Then, as people began to recognize the legitimacy of psychic phenomena, what had been thought of as a circus sideshow continued and grew more profitable. Scientists, government authorities, and psychologists all began to explore the field of psychic research, looking for the facts among the rumors. And through their work and the continuing emergence of proven psychics like myself, the field of psychic phenomena attained some recognition and respect. As proof of this, consider the book you have just read: Fifteen years ago, no publisher would even have considered marketing such a book.

What will be the outcome of this newfound discovery that we psychics are authentic? What role will psychic phenomena play in our future? In my opinion, the effects will be positive—and the new role we will play will be significant.

First, the number of people who are psychic will increase. As society continues to change its attitude toward psychics, more people—especially younger people—will be free to develop and recognize their gifts without fear of suspicion or condemnation from their peers. For my sister's children, for example, it will be far easier to continue developing their psychic abilities than it was for me. And, hopefully, the pressures that forced my mother and sister to abandon their gifts won't take such a heavy toll on the next generation of gifted young people.

Psychics have already begun to grow in number. I think it would be reasonable to estimate that during the next twenty years, they will triple in number. What effect will this increase have? Well, for one thing, it will give scientists and others involved in the study of parapsychology a greater opportunity to test and experiment. With so many more subjects available, psychic phenomena can begin to be explored in depth.

The most interesting part of this scientific study will involve young psychics. Just as doctors study the developmental process of average children in order to understand the human personality, so scientists will watch the progress of a gifted child as he or she grows in power and ability—and through this kind of study, some definite answer about the how and why of psychic power will be found.

The Beginning of a New Era

Then, in time, major breakthroughs will occur. Science will be able to show exactly how the psychic person can use his or her mind to see into the future. The magical, hocus-pocus elements will finally be removed, and psychic phenomena will be seen as a complex but understandable human activity.

These scientific breakthroughs will take time. But because of the meticulous nature of scientific research and testing, the eventual results will be undeniable.

We will discover many mental functions unheard of before now. Scientific research will find that virtually every human being is capable of precognition and ESP. Methods and devices may even be created to allow the average person to experience psychic power.

Though it may sound surprising, one effect of this breakthrough will be the return of many people to a deep religious faith: Once the tricks and illusions are put aside, once we stop looking to contact the dead or look into the world of afterlife, then psychic phenomena will be viewed not as witchcraft or mysticism but as concrete proof of the role of God in our lives. When we realize that a world *does* exist beyond that which we can see, and that this world is not one of superstition and ghosts and goblins, we will begin to appreciate the one loving God who looks over us all.

Albert Einstein was once asked if his discoveries had affected his belief in God. It was expected that a man who had spent his life looking for logical explanations for what had long been considered miracles might tend to be an atheist. But Einstein did not connect increased knowledge with decreased faith in God's existence. He said that his discoveries had not convinced him that God did not exist—quite the opposite. The more he learned, Einstein said, the more he realized he did not know. In much the same way, the breakthrough that lies ahead in the field of psychic research will lead to a renaissance of deep religious feeling.

These new understandings will have many positive effects on the world community. In time I believe that psychic phenomena will help bring peace to the world. Through a greater understanding of who and what we are, a better relationship will be created among nations.

This will take many, many years, however. In the meantime, I think we can expect to see people and governments using the psychic revolution to their own advantage. Psychic power will soon be considered a new weapon. People like myself will be used to spy on the operations of foreign governments, and within the next few years, I believe you can expect to see psychic warfare.

No great mental ability is needed to predict this astounding future government interest in psychic phenomena—it has already begun. But in the future, when there will be many new psychics around and major new discoveries that will, in effect, harness their powers, governments will be tempted to use people like me for less than honorable activities. With any luck, this phase of revolution will not last very long.

Psychics in Business

The business community, already deeply involved in the use of psychics, will find new tasks for us as well. If you can imagine what the government might do with a controllable psychic, you can begin to guess what nasty tricks business might come up with. In comparison to what we can expect in the future, corporate spying of the kind I once did will seem like child's play.

But something will come to prevent this situation from getting out of hand. I cannot say exactly what it will be, but some force—perhaps the will of God—will stop man from abusing psychics and harming himself. In much the same way, not all people will develop psychic power, even though we all may have the potential.

In fact, I believe the science-fiction image of an advanced people communicating without words is a relatively accurate picture of a stage mankind will reach one day. But this will not come any more quickly than it can be handled. The progress will be slow and steady, and advances will not come out of schedule with man's growing responsibility. I don't believe God will permit a small belligerent nation to use psychic gifts to the detriment of mankind as a whole. Somehow, some force will regulate the progress of this psychic revolution so that the outcome will be an improvement of life, and not destruction.

A Race of Psychics?

Although we may never become a race of psychics, I believe that in the future, all men will slowly find their mental powers heightened. The first phase of this development has already taken place. More and more people have learned the importance of self-knowledge, and many of us have begun to take a holistic approach to spiritual and physical health. Through continued growing awareness man will find himself more in touch with his own mind, and he will profit more from his own knowledge.

An area that fascinates many people, including myself, is

that of telekinesis—the ability to move or affect objects using mental power alone. You've probably seen one of the many horror movies that have come out on this topic. Unfortunately these movies reflect the attitudes of most people, who are more interested in hocus-pocus than in scientific realities.

I do not know what role telekinesis will play in the future; I cannot even say with certainty that this phenomenon exists. I have read many reports on the subject, particularly on Uri Geller, whose powers—if real—are absolutely amazing. But this is not an area in which I have personal experience, so it is hard for me to predict how telekinesis will change our future lives.

Certainly, if people with telekinetic powers do exist, and these powers are strengthened in the future, they could have tremendous potential to do good for man—just as there is a horrible possibility that they could cause harm and destruction.

The Psychic Revolution has already begun. The long-overdue arrival of recognition and respect accorded major psychics like Edgar Cayce was the first step. The next was the growing interest in psychic phenomena among the general public in the past decade. The third advance will be a tremendous increase in the number of legitimate psychics. From then on, the future will largely shape itself. Psychic powers will be more sharply defined and developed, and the nature of our understanding of ourselves and our universe will be transformed.

The New Frontier

I believe that the area of psychic phenomena—from ESP to clairvoyance or precognition—is the major frontier facing mankind in the years to come. Rather than finding new lands to conquer, we will explore our inner minds. We may find the true fountain of youth within our own souls. And the riches and wealth we will discover there will be greater than all the gold of the ancient Incas. I can think of no other area that offers a greater potential for good than that of the human mind. Once we have unlocked its secrets, we can begin to understand ourselves. From there we can work toward solving our problems—from the personal to the global.

Within your lifetime, you can expect to see amazing changes in the world of parapsychology. What is now considered to be unproven—or just a possibility—will eventually be accepted as fact. The people now considered phonies will be accepted as revered professionals and experts.

The change has already begun. You are living through one of the biggest revolutions in the history of mankind. And you will be a part of this change. Through your acceptance of what others consider impossible, you are leading the vanguard of this psychic revolution.

Keep believing as you do. Someday everyone will know you were right.

18
Dealing With Your Personal Fate

The other morning I sat down in my apartment to begin working on this, the final chapter of this book. I knew what I wanted to talk about: destiny and fate, how they affect us, and how we can learn to make them work for us.

I soon found myself thinking about my own destiny, as I often do. Sometimes I dream about what may happen in the years ahead. But at other times I think only of the next few days or hours. The future—both distant and immediate—is where our destiny lies. Fate shapes not only who and where you will be ten years from now, but also ten hours from now.

I paused in my mental journey and called a friend. "Hi, Jane. This is Shawn."

"Hi, Shawn. I was just going to call you."

"Listen, let's make it lunch on Friday."

Jane paused. I could hear her thinking. "Shawn . . . how did you know I wanted to see you this week?" As a psychic, I am somewhat aware of what my future holds at almost every given moment. Even though it might be vague, I have some idea of what is going to happen next. To a certain degree, I know my destiny.

But what *is* this thing we refer to as fate? Is there really a plan, an order to our lives? Does some outer force control us in unseen ways? How is our destiny shaped by God's plan, or the planets, or our earlier lives? What makes your fate different from mine?

And how can you get in touch with your fate and let it help you through life?

Without question, some very real force pushes us in a chosen direction, controls the apparent "coincidences" and "lucky breaks" we stumble on from time to time. Whether you know it or not, whether you observe or ignore it, fate is shaping every aspect of your existence.

If you prefer to guess at the source of fate and destiny, I will not discourage you. The point is not where fate begins, but rather where it leads. Some people spend their lives struggling against their destiny. They try to move in directions not intended by fate. The final result of such a battle can be devastating. And as you can guess, destiny will not lose the fight; only the individual stands to lose.

Fighting fate leads to many things, none of them pleasant or beneficial. Disappointment, failure, anxiety, depression, and heartache come to him who struggles against his destiny. Consider the talented painter, musician, or writer who does not pursue his or her art. Instead of going into the risky career of the artist, this person decides to seek security in business. But the artist who denies his talent will probably make a very poor businessman. And he will be forever frustrated, longing for the fulfillment he experienced when practicing his true vocation.

By learning to work *with* fate instead of against it, you can avoid this kind of mistake. You can discover what you really should be doing with your life and stop wasting the precious time you have on this earth. You can get what you want from life, move in the right directions, and make the right choices in love and career matters, making the most of your life and existence.

Make no mistake: Fate affects everything you do, guiding you through every day. Eventually it controls us completely. Even when you *think* you're acting independently, making your own decisions, you are really being moved by your destiny.

But how can you find your fate and get in touch with your destiny? The answer is easy to say, but not as easy to perform. You must start looking inside yourself, listening to your own attitudes and feelings. And you must stop living your life according to the attitudes and feelings of others.

Most people live someone *else's* destiny. You serve your employer faithfully, making lots of money for him. Whose fate is being fulfilled? Not your own, most likely! The same is true of loved ones, children, and friends. All too often you serve to bring *their* fates to reality, while ignoring your own.

Living to fulfill the expectations of others is fighting fate, which brings only failure. You must begin to live by your *own* expectations. Your role in this world, your nature and personality are completely unique. Only you can truly uncover the plan that is guiding you from day to day. Only you can find out what your own fate will be. Do, think, feel, and say what *you* want, not what others would *like* you to do. Take your life where you want it to go. Those feelings you sense are the voice of your own destiny, trying to help you make the right decisions. Follow them, and you will be striding into your life. Ignore them, and you will be at odds with the master plan.

In this chapter I'll show you how to find the pattern of your life to this point. In this pattern you will see the hand of fate working in unison with your personality.

As you read earlier in this book, I spent a large portion of my life battling my destiny. When I was younger, I knew how most people felt about psychic phenomena, so naturally I did everything in my power to deny that I was psychic. I took on others' attitudes and ideas so strongly that I was willing to live a lie, to spend my entire existence denying what I truly was.

Though I fought the battle hard, I couldn't submerge my true nature below a show of conformity and apparent normalcy. I was not average. I could not be like everyone else. Finally, in a way, my fate simply threw itself upon me and left me no alternative to follow. The psychic dreams and visions never really went away, and in time they actually began to grow stronger. I had no choice.

Forced to admit my destiny, I was actually lucky. My purpose and powers were so strong I could not fight them successfully. But most people don't enjoy this rare opportunity. For many, it is completely possible to devote an entire lifetime to the denial of self. You may not be living your true destiny right now. Through your own determination and the pressure you feel from others, you may have the ability to completely suppress your true nature.

I can promise you that it is possible to get in touch with your own fate and make it work for you. The key—honest self-examination—is not an easy process, but the degree of difficulty is different for every individual. I have met small children who are in complete accord with their inner selves, completely in harmony with their destiny. And by the same token, I have met adults who have no idea who they are or where they're going.

The first step is perhaps the most difficult on the road to dealing with fate. It is to *stop* living according to other people's words and promises and to start following your own instincts. If you have a certain intuitive feeling about something, follow it. Even if others warn against it and assure you how wrong you are, your internal feelings and instincts are a message to you from a force deep within. The signal telling you which path to take, and what to do next, is the voice of your inner self, your subconscious—your destiny.

When you start following and trusting your own feelings, you will soon begin to see just how much control you can have over your life. You will discover that your insights are more often correct than others' advice and promises. You will feel renewed strength and power over the forces that try to move you against your better judgment. This force and power comes directly from learning to work in cooperation *with* fate instead of against it.

You may be nervous about taking such bold action—I was, too, for many, many years! But think about it this way: You are an intelligent person. You have had many good and bad experiences in your lifetime. No matter what your age, you have been exposed to many things, and you've learned a lot. What makes you think someone else knows more than you do? How can another person know your own needs better than you yourself? Whose judgment can you trust more than your own?

Following your instincts *seems* frightening and dangerous only because other people have forced you to think this way. It is external pressure, the attitudes and expectations of others, that make you doubt your own feelings. This nervousness is an example of how you are living someone else's fate.

Right now, I want to try a little exercise. You are going to make a brief overview of your life.

Get a piece of paper and a pencil, and try to write a simple schedule for the major events in your life. You can do this year by year. For each year, make a note about these three things: what you were doing, how you felt about it, and what you *really* wanted to do.

A typical listing might be: "Age 16. In school. Hated it. Wanted to move away from home soon." Make some kind of note like this for every year of your life—including the early years when you were only four or five years old.

As you come closer and closer to the present, this list will begin to show you exactly how you got to where you are today. Perhaps you had a job offer, and quickly accepted. Soon you were pursuing a career in this field—maybe a line of work you never had the least interest in. Perhaps you had a brief, unsuccessful romance that left you depressed and led to some major event in your life. Whatever the details, you can see how you have moved from one point to another, from one year to the next.

Many of us are like the metal balls in a pinball machine, bouncing from one place to another, scoring points now and then, and ultimately heading toward the bottom and the end of the game. And yet there is a strong element of personal choice. You do not simply bounce around, you go from one place to another voluntarily. You *choose* to take that job, get married, drop out of school, or whatever it is you have done. It was your decision. So to a large degree you have already shaped your existence.

The question is, Did you know what you were doing? Did you make those decisions with an objective, a well-planned pattern in mind? Probably not! While you went of your own choice, you still bounced to some degree. Why? Because you followed the words of others while ignoring your own instincts.

When your list is complete, examine it thoroughly from time to time for the next few weeks. Think about it often. Look for patterns. See if you can find a point where your life turned around, where you departed from your earlier plans and began a whole new life-style. More than likely, this is where you began to fight your fate.

But, on the other hand, this might actually be the point where you joined with destiny. It is a completely personal matter.

This chart shows *your* life, and I cannot tell you exactly how to interpret it.

Again, the key is your feelings. As you analyze your chart, pay close attention to your instinctive feelings about the events of your life. Are you happy these things happened to you? What do you regret? Where do you *feel* you went wrong? This is a subjective, personal matter. You must struggle with it on your own. Based on the chart, see if you have any instincts about where you will be next year . . . or the year after that . . . or five or ten years from today. And always listen to that first, that original notion that enters your mind. Chances are, this is the voice of fate.

Perhaps you don't like the direction in which your life seems to be going. If not, why? You must ask yourself what bothers you. How would you like to change? When you find answers, take action on them. Don't listen to others who may try to stop you. Be strong, follow your feelings, and you will be on your way to dealing with your own destiny.

Your horoscope can be very useful in the search. It will tell you many things about your personality and help you understand who you really are. I believe very deeply in the powers of astrology and think that if you are able to get a reliable astrologer to draw an accurate chart, its predictions for your future will not be incorrect. You can rely on that chart to tell you almost exactly what will happen to you in the days ahead. With this information, you can begin to get a better idea of your own fate and destiny, and what lies in your future.

A professional psychic can also be very helpful in your search for your true fate. If you know a psychic or can find one, visit this person right away. Tell them exactly what you want to know. Ask them to help you discover your destiny.

Then follow their advice to the best of your powers.

When you begin to know more about who you are and start to take hold of your life, you can slowly begin to incorporate other people's attitudes and ideas again. The point is not to accept them blindly as you did before, to the exclusion of your own feelings, but rather to examine each piece of information or advice carefully, evaluating its truthfulness and how it relates to you. If these ideas are in keeping with your instincts, you can use them in your life. If the words of others go directly against what you know in your heart, listen to yourself and ignore the others.

In the long run, you will find a happy balance between outer and inner forces. It *is* possible to get along in this world and meet the demands of others without sacrificing your integrity, ignoring your feelings, and fighting against your fate. You can learn to live in harmony with a force you cannot defeat: your unique and undeniable destiny.

Try as many people do, it's really impossible to make your destiny go away. All you do is make it more difficult to get to where you are eventually going. Sometimes when people try to deny fate, they put up a tremendous struggle and manage to negate many of the effects of destiny. The result is that nothing happens at all! No progress is made in any direction.

But for most people, fate simply remains hidden, waiting below the surface to show its powers. If you are moving in a direction that leads away from your fate, many surprising events can be awaiting you. The outcome is uncertain, and there is surely a large degree of danger involved.

By seeing where you have come from in life, and knowing where you are probably going, you can make the decisions that will bring happiness and success. You can help your fate and destiny do the work they were intended for, and can help fulfill that master plan.

In my life, I have been lucky enough to see my fate and move toward it. I am living my destiny right now, this very moment. Writing this book is part of my fate. I truly believe that you and I were destined to be communicating in this fashion.

I want you to find your fate and all the happiness it can bring. Consider carefully the ideas we've discussed in this chapter, and in this entire book. Consider these words carefully, evaluating them against your own ideas, feelings, and intuitions. I think you will find they are in close harmony with your own feelings and instincts.

Whatever road you take through this world, walk it in your own shoes. Live your *own* life. Do what you think is right, not what others tell you to do, and your journey through this life will be more happy and successful.

Index